Holistech

A Philosopher's Playbook on the Hidden Art of Flourishing

Aida I. Askry, Ph.D.

Evertree Publishing
www.evertreepublishing.com

Copyright © 2023
All rights reserved.

First Edition
Published 2023

Orange Geometry cover drawing by Nathalie Strassburg
www.nathaliestrassburg.com

ISBN 978-1-7321526-2-5

Printed in the United States of America

www.holistech.club

Contents

Introduction   1

01 **Physical Wellness and Mental Health**   15

02 **Peak Cognitive Performance**   37

03 **The Art of Aging Well and the Secrets of Timeless Beauty**   71

04 **Personal and Organizational Development**   83

05 **Authentic Human Connection and Development**   89

HOLIS**TECH**

Introduction

As humans, we often grapple with the inevitability of change.

Though it's a constant presence in our lives, we resist it, attempting to exert control over our environment regardless of how successful or unsuccessful we may be.

In a future that is closer than we might imagine, the boundaries between human performance and technology will begin to blur and eventually dissolve. We stand on the precipice of a transformative era—a time in which the practices of holistic wellness will intertwine with the advances of technology. This integration will trigger shifts in the paradigm of human potential, redefining well-being and how we perceive it. This imminent change will challenge our traditional notions and usher in a radically different perspective on health and human performance.

This is not just an evolution—it's a revolution in the way we live.

HOLISTECH

Human performance is multifaceted. It includes cognitive function, emotional balance, physical prowess, and spiritual well-being. We often associate human performance with extraordinary feats, but its true essence lies beyond the fleeting moment.

It encompasses a consistent pursuit of excellence in every facet of our lives: in confronting vulnerabilities, challenging limits, and committing to ongoing growth and learning. Health and well-being are not reducible to cholesterol levels, lack of disease, or numbers on a scale. Vibrant health is an all-encompassing state of flourishing, including physical vitality, mental clarity, emotional stability, and a profound sense of inner peace and contentment. Caring for our health involves nurturing our bodies, minds, and souls and acknowledging their interconnectedness.

Vibrant health is a state of all-encompassing flourishing. It depends on the ongoing integration of these interconnected dimensions to our being—the physical, the mental, the emotional, the spiritual.

Embracing this has an impact on every element of our daily routine. It changes food, rest, stress management, and connections with others and ourselves. It entails embracing a way of life that nourishes us on all levels and makes us resilient in the face of life's inevitable ups and downs.

When we approach this as an act of self-care and self-compassion, we nurture an intimate relationship with ourselves. Self-care is not about hollow self-indulgence, but about making choices that honor our true nature, and align us with our vision for the future. Self-compassion involves extending kindness and understanding to ourselves, especially in times of failure or struggle.

We are a masterpiece in progress. Every step, if taken with vision, should bring us closer to our highest potential.

Achieving and maintaining optimal well-being is a deliberate and continuous journey, an act of love and respect for ourselves. It is not a finish line to cross or a box to tick off, but rather a lifestyle to embrace. It is a journey of continuous growth and self-discovery. It can be challenging to admit that we don't have all the answers.

We are finite beings. The optimal path is never clear. Life is filled with the unexpected and the inexplicable, paradigm-shifting events whose significance is often clear only in retrospect years later.

"I invite you to explore with me the myriad topics that represent the integration of human performance and current technology."

HOLISTECH

My goal here is not to sway you either for or against the impending revolutionary advances in technology and artificial intelligence that will affect human performance. Rather, I am offering an open invitation for you to reflect on your stance and reconsider your aspirations. We're living through a moment that presents a unique opportunity for reevaluation. We must decide which aspects of our lives to enhance and carry forward, and which to leave behind. Many of these decisions are not entirely within our control, but choosing how to navigate these changes is our responsibility nonetheless.

Responsibility. Isn't that one of the conclusions all our greatest thinkers come to, in considering our human finitude? You can either embrace it, and embrace responsibility; or you can throw up your hands, give in to bitterness, and suffer nonetheless.

There's a story we tell ourselves, about who we are and what we stand for, about what we've experienced and what it means. Central to this story is the concept of the 'self.' Some refer to this as the ego, while in certain psychology texts you might come across the term 'conceptualized self.' This self-narrative we spin follows us through every stage and mission of our lives. Understanding the construction of this 'self' involves examining the building blocks from which it is formed.

These building blocks are shaped by culture, upbringing, beliefs, education, and media exposure. These cultural reference points provide standards for not only norms and behaviors but the very way we perceive and categorize the world around us. Our parents instill values in us. Media and socialization influence our perceptions and aspirations. How we absorb and respond to these building blocks forms the basis of our human potential and performance. Yet the decision lies with us: we can internalize these building blocks—allowing them to define us subconsciously—or we can choose what to preserve and what to discard.

As we anticipate the convergence of health and technology in the landscape of human well-being, this choice becomes ever more critical.

With this understanding, I invite you to explore with me the myriad topics that represent the integration of human performance and current technology. As you traverse these pages, I encourage you to evaluate and connect with the ideas presented, observing the stories and real-life situations that arise and fall around you. I trust that through this exploration you will gain a deeper understanding of yourself and your potential, enabling you to navigate through life with grace.

HOLIS**TECH**

The Journey

My tale begins in the bustling cityscape of Tehran, Iran. The city is a tapestry of historical convergence, a labyrinth of culture. It is a whirlpool of paradoxical emotions. This was where I opened my eyes to the world.

I grew up in the 90s, a delicate era for Iran. We were suffering a regime change and the aftereffects of war. As a child, the complexities of this political environment were utterly lost on me; but they formed the landscape of my existence, and that of my family.

From a young age, the enigma of human potential ignited my fascination. I was intrigued by our ability to question, to dream, and to constantly redefine the boundaries of existence. My interest lay in understanding what gave our lives depth, meaning, and quality.

In the post-revolution era, my family's belief system and religious views were met with disdain and disapproval by the new order. Branded as infidels, we found ourselves in the grip of an omnipresent fear. We existed in a perpetual state of 'fight or flight.' Our home was all we knew—we tried, of course, to cling to the good and simply shelter from the bad. Like countless others across the globe, however, we found ourselves sliding down an aching, painful, lonely slope towards flight. Ultimately, we had to leave.

Our journey to freedom was a fragmented one. The political and financial barriers to family immigration forced us to scatter like seeds in the wind, my parents forced to support each of us as we left our homeland behind. Through this experience, we bore witness to the unwavering resilience of the human spirit.

Growing up, my family had always encouraged us to question the status quo, to push the boundaries of our understanding, and to relentlessly seek our personal truth. We held this resolve close in our hearts, an ember in the chilling winds of scrutiny and disdain. Despite the ongoing harassment and discrimination, my parents taught us to recognize the intrinsic beauty and goodness within every individual, regardless of their faith or background. Our home was open to all forms of spiritual and social expression, allowing us to explore and appreciate the full landscape of possibility when it came to finding meaning and purpose in life.

At sixteen I penned my first book, which I called Rebirth of Perception, a youthful exposition of radical thinking, philosophical debates, and spiritual exploration. I urged readers to embrace their innate curiosity and to challenge the foundations of their beliefs. Looking back, I'm thankful it wasn't published there and then. Its far-out ideas could have led to extreme legal consequences for my family and me. (Maybe reading about Joan of Arc as a teenager wasn't the best idea after all!) was told it was too revolutionary for the establishment. It struck fear into the hearts of those who wished to confine us to accepted thought. It was unpublishable. I took this message as my cue, finally recognizing it was time to choose 'flight' over 'fight.'

Carrying with me my free spirit and unquenchable curiosity, I embarked on a solo journey that spanned across continents and years, finally landing in the United States. My goal, of course, was to pursue my dreams. I had ambitions and aspirations, but the path to realizing them was undefined. My curiosity pushed me to explore various human experiences, from ancient esoteric practices to cutting-edge scientific breakthroughs that are redefining our nature of reality and human potential.

With a seemingly infinite array of disciplines to study, I 'narrowed' my focus to philosophy, psychology, and neuroscience. The financial requirements of pursuing a doctorate in these fields didn't deter me. I was committed to parallel self-education and personal growth, regardless of the formal structures in place.

Over the span of eight years—while advancing my knowledge in the empirical fields of psychology and neuroscience—I managed to conclude a doctorate in philosophy, with a focus on the mind-body connection through research. I had the good fortune to explore ancient practices like yoga, qi gong, meditation, and breathwork under the mentorship of esteemed teachers from around the globe.

In my journey of exploration, I realized that academic specialization has a tendency to limit one's perspective, hindering the ability to make connections across diverse fields. Instead of becoming a specialist in one discipline, I made a conscious decision to nurture a multi-disciplinary perspective, to pursue breadth over depth. This decision was a challenge to the academic status quo. It demanded effort, and it isolated me somewhat; but it enabled me to traverse my own unique academic and professional landscape.

As I navigated through these fascinating intersections of disciplines, the seeds of my childhood fascination began to blossom. The diversity of my experiences and profound human interactions weaved into complex and beautiful patterns; a kaleidoscope through which I could more fully appreciate the depth of human potential.

Today I can say I have engaged authentically with the intricacies of human experience across a breathtaking spectrum of lives and stories, each unique and inspiring in its own way. I have encountered people from every conceivable walk of life, each person with a tale of their own, each story a testament to the strength and resilience of the human spirit

Through my journey, I have learned that the process of self-discovery and growth is not a solitary endeavor but a dance that takes place at the intersection of personal experiences and the shared wisdom of humanity. This path of learning is not a solitary trek into the wilderness but a shared journey on which we inspire each other to reach higher and dive deeper.

In retrospect, my story is less about overcoming a daunting past and more about a humble journey toward understanding, curiosity, and personal growth. Each step, from the vibrant lanes of Tehran to the scholarly hubs of the United States, has influenced my evolution. Today, I stand with humility, a seeker of ancient wisdom, a participant in the evolving world of technology, and a steadfast believer in the untapped potential that resides in every human being.

My journey is one of resilience, curiosity, and determination. I've learned that even in the face of adversity, the human spirit thrives on the pursuit of knowledge and the exploration of the world within us and around us. My life serves as a testament to the beauty of diversity, the power of curiosity, and the joy of lifelong learning.

Even today, as I delve deeper into the mysteries of human performance and human potential, I am continually amazed by the diverse mosaic of experiences that life has to offer. My journey continues, and with every step, I am reminded of the profound connections we all share in our pursuit of understanding and growth.

HOLIS**TECH**

The Voyage

In the prime of my 20s, I embarked on an extraordinary professional voyage, embracing the role of a personal development and wellness consultant. It was a path that allowed me to explore the intersection of various disciplines, leveraging my multifaceted education and experiences to guide others toward realizing their full potential and nurturing their overall well-being.

One of my most profound realizations in those early years was this: the conventional model of human potential and well-being—both physical and mental—often operates in a reactive rather than proactive manner. We tend to overlook our health and wellness until something goes awry, then rush to find a quick fix and return to a somewhat passive status quo.

Over my decade of working with professional athletes, executives, and individuals in recovery, I've seen firsthand that this reactive mindset can cause more harm than good. Most of us seek help only to get back to our pre-symptomatic state, rather than genuinely wanting to understand the root cause of our issues, and aiming to improve our overall well-being.

When we view wellness as merely the absence of illness, or a state where symptoms are kept at bay, we miss a crucial aspect of the equation. Having worked with over 7,500 individuals, I can say with confidence that genuine happiness and well-being stem from a deeper desire to cultivate a flourishing life, rather than merely striving to avoid discomfort and pain.

So, how does one get from lack-of-illness to wellness and beyond?

This is where positive psychology comes into play, introducing the theory of happiness and well-being. Dr. Martin Seligman's PERMA model offers a captivating roadmap for human flourishing, extending beyond mere wellness. PERMA represents Positive emotions, Engagement (or experiencing a state of flow), Relationships, Meaning, and Accomplishments. Dr. Seligman found that embracing these five elements frequently paves the way to a life characterized by happiness, well-being, and true flourishing.

Empowered with this theory, is it now possible to shift our focus from merely overcoming illness to instead pursuing a life of flourishing?

It is—but the journey towards happiness and well-being requires constant attention, perhaps more than attention than we offered in our state of illness. This is not a reactionary 'once in a while' routine, but something we want to develop and sustain in life.

HOLISTECH

So how can we transition from a state of mere wellness to a state of true flourishing?

Today, with ongoing innovations in holistic wellness, I'm hopeful about a smooth transition. There are countless organizations, researchers, and innovators harnessing the power of technology to not only alleviate symptoms but to also gain a deeper understanding of the 'how' and 'why' of the physical and mental ailments that afflict us. We are witnessing an unprecedented integration of advanced technology in well-being practices. This union serves to augment our physical and cognitive abilities, deepen our understanding of our minds and bodies, and provide innovative ways to prevent, diagnose, and treat diseases. Wearable fitness trackers, telemedicine, AI-powered diagnostics, personalized skin care, supplements, and medicine—these are just a few examples of the convergence of technology and health that is revolutionizing our lives.

Picture this: an AI-powered health app that not only tracks your physical activity but also offers personalized nutrition advice, tailored physical exercises, and comprehensive mental health support. It could learn from your unique biofeedback and provide recommendations specifically designed for your individual needs and preferences. This remarkable fusion of health practices and advanced technology has the power to redefine the essence of human performance and reshape our perception of well-being.

Of course, there are skeptics who argue that relying heavily on technology may diminish the human aspect of health and performance. They are not entirely wrong.

Technology is indeed a tool, and it cannot replace the importance of human connection, strategic thinking, and empathy. Remember: this book is about the visionary and holistic integration of tech with spirituality, with diet, with psychology, and with all these other things so many brilliant people have been studying for generations. Everything is meant to be.

Throughout my personal and professional experiences (which I will share shortly), I have come to believe that maintaining a balanced perspective is crucial as we navigate this transition. By acknowledging the value of both the human touch and technological advancements, we can strive to create a performance and development system that is more personalized, preventive, and empowering than ever before.

It is admittedly important to address the ethical implications that arise from the use of technology in human performance. There are concerns surrounding privacy, equal access, responsible development and utilization, and the impact on employment in the health and wellness industry. We must strive to leverage technology in a manner that respects individual privacy, promotes equity, and safeguards the well-being of all.

As we navigate this transformative epoch, I encourage you to ponder our ever-shifting landscapes. I must underscore the idea that this technological metamorphosis isn't about completely ousting the old to make way for the new. Rather, it's about harmoniously blending the learned wisdom of the past with the potential of the future. It's about dreaming of the advancements that can come with creativity, openness, and the recognition of our nature.

HOLIS**TECH**

01
Optimal Physical Wellness and Mental Health

> We first make our habits, and then our habits make us.

John Dryden

HOLIS**TECH**

In my 20s, I was always intrigued by the focus adults placed on their health and wellness, even when they seemed perfectly healthy. I observed how, as we age, we often become more invested in maintaining our well-being and controlling our environment. At that time though, I didn't fully grasp the significance of simple everyday habits like getting enough sleep, eating well, monitoring health performance records, and overall self-care. My energy was largely channeled into juggling full-time work and full-time school. I often neglected my own well-being but, being young, would always manage to bounce back without even really noticing.

As I transitioned into my 30s however, I experienced an increase in self-awareness. Perhaps it was having fewer commitments. I finally had time to slow down and reflect on my routine. I started to notice patterns: a lack of good sleep would render me sluggish and irritable the next day. It made it difficult to recall information for work, and induced a general sense of indifference towards life. If I didn't nourish myself, or made sudden changes to my diet, my body would react almost immediately with changes in appetite, bloating, or skin irritation. Sometimes I was besieged by all these symptoms simultaneously. It was quite the rollercoaster!

It became clear that while I might have enjoyed robust health in my 20s, sustaining it into my 30s would require conscientious changes to combat the inexorable march of time. It was time to reassess my lifestyle choices.

At my subsequent annual health check-up, I voiced my concerns to my doctor. She assured me that my test results were fine; everything was within the normal range. Yet I couldn't help but question this. How could everything remain the same when I felt and saw periodic changes? Could a standard test with a generic "normal" result range genuinely describe my individual and optimal health? While I understood the relevance of these tests for diagnostic purposes, their role in assessing my overall well-being seemed less accurate.

A few years later, while working as a wellness consultant at a functional medicine practitioner's office, I had the opportunity to engage with patients in depth. I learned more about the distinction between 'good' health and optimal health. Being within the normal range for certain markers didn't necessarily imply feeling my best. For instance, my hormone levels might be normal for the average person, but not necessarily for my specific circumstances and needs.

I think of my friend Amy, a fitness instructor. She began noticing unusual weight gain and fatigue that disrupted her daily routines. Initial blood tests by her general practitioner showed that her TSH (Thyroid Stimulating Hormone) levels were within the normal range. But given her symptoms, she decided to see an endocrinologist for a more comprehensive evaluation. The specialist assessed not just the TSH but also her Free T4 and Free T3 levels. Even though her TSH was in range, her Free T4 was on the lower end and her Free T3 was suboptimal.

The endocrinologist explained that sometimes a person can have a normal TSH but still have a form of subclinical hypothyroidism or thyroid conversion issues, especially if T3, the active form of thyroid hormone, is low. Amy was then placed on a treatment plan, including a specific T3 medication, and over time her energy levels improved and she returned to her active self. Similarly, while my hormone levels might appear 'normal' by general standards, they may not be ideal for my distinct needs and conditions.

With a fresh focus on pinpointing individual patterns and needs, I pondered how I could harness the insights from functional medicine practitioners without diminishing the value of traditional medicine, with its proven efficacy in curing illnesses and relieving pain for countless patients. Once again, I recognized the importance of an open mind and a multidisciplinary perspective in the pursuit of good health and happiness.

Throughout this chapter we will explore the elements that I've found essential for maximizing overall health and wellness. I'll share the techniques that have been most successful with my clients, and the technologies that are making this journey ever easier and more fine-tuned.

Sleep and Physical Recovery

As a young child, whenever I was ailing, our family doctor would expertly diagnose and address the problem at hand. But our wellness education stopped short there. The subsequent steps (recovery, treatment, and potential side effects) were never discussed. That changed when I embraced the holistic health model.

When I encountered an infection later in life, my functional medicine practitioner painted a broader picture. I advised to counterbalance the antibiotics' impact with prebiotics and probiotics. I was taught the importance of rest and high-quality sleep, particularly the concept of sleep pressure. At that time the term was unfamiliar, let alone its connection to my overall health and recovery.

Sleep pressure, or sleep drive, is the fascinating biological phenomenon by which, the longer we stay awake, the greater our need for sleep. It's a dance between brain activity and the accumulation of a byproduct called adenosine. The longer we're awake, the more adenosine piles up, increasing the urge to sleep. As we sleep, adenosine levels recede and we rejuvenate.

Our sleep cycle is a symphony conducted by sleep pressure and our internal circadian rhythm. When they are in sync, we enjoy refreshing sleep at night and alert wakefulness during the day.

Disruptions in this harmony lead to sleep disorders like insomnia, delayed sleep phase syndrome, advanced sleep phase syndrome, non-24-hour sleep-wake disorder, and irregular sleep-wake rhythm. These disorders not only affect our nighttime rest but can also impact our daily functioning, mood, and overall health.

Countering sleep pressure, there's another fundamental process at play: the fight-or-flight response, also known as the "acute stress response." A survival mechanism, it primes the body for quick action by releasing hormones like adrenaline and cortisol in response to perceived threats or stress. Chronic activation of this response can disrupt the balance between the sympathetic and parasympathetic nervous systems, leading to long-term physical and mental disruption.

The parasympathetic nervous system governs the rest and repair cycles in our body. During these periods of relaxation, we undergo vital processes like digestion, tissue repair, and immune system functioning.

I learned that sleep is the golden thread linking the fight-or-flight response, as well as the rest-and-repair cycles. Poor sleep can trigger inappropriate stress responses and disrupt vital restorative processes, leaving us vulnerable to a host of health issues. On the flip side, good sleep hygiene promotes a healthy interplay between the sympathetic and parasympathetic nervous systems. It fosters a state of balance, reduces chronic stress, and supports overall wellness.

Throughout my journey towards self-mastery and peak performance, I've come to profoundly respect the role of sleep. In a world that celebrates the hustle, I discovered that embracing deep and restful sleep is a true game-changer. By refining my nightly routines, I found that some simple yet impactful adjustments can make a world of difference: setting a consistent bedtime, steering clear of screens at least an hour before bed, engaging in a pre-sleep ritual like reading or meditating, and ensuring the bedroom is a sanctuary—cool, quiet, and dark. Remember: it's not just about fancy mattresses or the allure of habit-forming medications. It's about listening to our bodies and respecting our innate need for restoration. When we prioritize quality sleep, we don't just improve our nights. We supercharge our days with enhanced focus, creativity, and a palpable zest for life.

If there's one piece of advice to take to heart, it's this: honor your sleep, and watch the ripple effect it has on every facet of your existence.

HOLISTECH

Nutrition and Dietary Choices

Growing up, I primarily consumed a Mediterranean diet along with a mix of fresh vegetables, fruits, carbs, and meat. I don't recall our family doctor ever testing my blood for food sensitivities or suggesting what foods to eat based on my unique body. Being the youngest child at home often allowed me to imagine what my future health may look like based on my parents and siblings' state of well-being. Maybe I was looking for assurance, a familiar pattern I could predict and perhaps even plan on. But soon, it became evident that even though we all ate the same foods, our physical, mental, and emotional reactions to food differed.

Certain foods were beneficial for one of us but not for the others. My mother used to say one person's food could be another person's poison—an idea I often challenged when it meant I couldn't have more fresh walnuts and olives! So, she would carefully feed us and would go so far as to make a variety of meals each day to make sure we each had a proper meal and ate what was good for us. I clearly remember how some of our friends and relatives would make fun of our parents and blame them for spoiling us with too many options. In reality, my parents wanted us to protect our greatest wealth, our health, even if the family doctor didn't see the need to do so unless we were ill.

I can only assume I am far from the first throughout history to experience this brand of motherly love. There is a breadth of ancient and modern modalities which emphasize eating based on your unique constitution. For instance, Ayurvedic medicine claims that each person has a unique combination of three 'doshas,' (Vata, Pitta, and Kapha) which is determined at the moment of conception. Meanwhile, in Traditional Chinese Medicine, a person's unique mix of the five elements (Wood, Fire, Earth, Metal, and Water) is called a 'Five Element Constitution'. Most recently, the idea of 'eating for your blood type' has been proposed. One thing these systems all share is an emphasis on the uniqueness of each individual's nutritional needs—a stark contrast to a simplified 'food pyramid' or standard balanced plate.

Nowadays, despite having access to comprehensive personalized lab work, nutritional facts, wearable technology, and the modern health sciences, I still observe people making questionable choices while eating out or grocery shopping, loading their baskets with foods that would make most mothers cringe: sugar, alcohol, highly processed food, and even worse.

I began to question why we subject ourselves to such habits. Lack of knowledge or resources to learn about healthy eating and maintaining a healthy lifestyle was no longer a valid excuse. Why do we place so much emphasis on treating symptoms when they arise without also delving deeper into achieving and maintaining holistic well-being that can keep uncomfortable symptoms from appearing in the first place? Could technology help us raise our awareness, make better choices, form healthier habits, and stick with them for good? I sure hoped so!

Embracing the search for a deeper understanding of the nuanced relationship between my diet and overall health, I stumbled upon metabolic health tracker devices. These tools were revolutionary to me, offering an intimate window into the nuances of my body's metabolic responses to the foods I consumed, my eating habits, and even my activity levels. It's truly astonishing to witness firsthand how each individual's metabolism is as unique as their fingerprint. Every morsel we consume has the potential to either fuel or derail our body's complex processes, a reality these devices rendered visible.

Metabolic health, as I came to discover, isn't just about how many calories we burn. It encapsulates the broader understanding of how our bodies utilize the energy derived from different nutrients, especially carbohydrates and fats. For instance, some individuals have metabolisms that are adept at burning fats for energy, entering a state called ketosis more easily. In contrast, others may rely more heavily on carbohydrates as their primary energy source.

Through these devices, I was introduced to the concept of the 'fat burning zone' versus the 'carb burning zone.' These zones highlight the different intensities at which our body predominantly relies on fats or carbs for energy.

These gadgets use a special breathing test to measure the amount of CO_2 in your breath, which tells us if we're burning carbs or fats. You breathe in a certain amount of air, hold it for 10 seconds, and then breathe out. If there's a lot of CO_2, it means your body is burning carbs, and if there's a little, it means your body is burning fats. Understanding which zone I was in at any given time allowed me to make more informed choices about the types of food I consumed, aiming for an

HOLISTECH

optimal balance that my body responded to best.

The beauty of having access to this kind of information is that it adds another layer to the narrative of individualized health. No longer are we just talking about doshas, elements, or blood types; we are delving into real-time data about our metabolic functioning. This renewed perspective made me appreciate the potential of technology not just as an accessory, but as a guide on my journey towards better health. If utilized correctly, these advancements promise a future where our diet aligns seamlessly with our metabolic predispositions, championing a holistic health approach that emphasizes prevention over cure.

Fashion Choices

Throughout my experiences with diverse clients, I have observed a fascinating phenomenon surrounding clients and their fashion choices. Many people fail to recognize that their apparel can have a significant impact on well-being. This issue is particularly noticeable in the more active clients, who usually have an increased mindfulness for physical alignment, posture, and a generally heightened awareness of their body.

Health-conscious individuals often express concerns about persistent discomfort in necks, shoulders, legs, or lower backs. They complain about feelings of muscular tension, tightness, or joint pain. As a result they are frequently seeking supplements, massage therapy, and other methods to improve their physical performance. I've begun to realize that a startling degree of discomfort is brought about due simply to choices of clothing and footwear.

I notice an abundance of outfits that are excessively form-fitting, offering little to no range of motion, locking the body away from natural movement. Footwear is a massive contributor. Much of the urban population alternates between dress shoes with a narrow toe box, and padded sports shoes that seemed to get fluffier each season. Many women I speak with spend more hours in high heels than they do barefoot. Seeing this, it doesn't surprise me when even my younger clients tell me they suffered chronic aching joints.

Aching joints, misalignment, and accelerated aging are inevitable, with these choices.

During our discussions, I would often be asked about my own fashion choices. To their surprise, I would always be wearing my professional attire that was completely suitable for movement while maintaining a formal appearance. My choice of footwear? Barefoot shoes, which offered complete comfort and natural movement.

My journey towards embracing comfortable and natural footwear began in my early twenties, driven largely by my yoga practice. An awareness of foot strength, stability, and flexibility made me realize the vital role footwear plays in overall health. I noticed a stark contrast between practicing yoga on a firm floor versus on a thick, cushioned mat. When I practiced barefoot on a harder surface, my joints functioned better, and I experienced increased balance and control.

HOLISTECH

Taking my quest beyond the yoga mat, I discovered barefoot shoes or minimalist shoes. "Zero drop" barefoot shoes are minimalist footwear designed to replicate the sensation of walking barefoot by eliminating the height difference between the heel and forefoot, promoting a natural and even footstrike. These shoes not only encourage better posture but may also reduce the risk of certain foot and leg issues. They also enhance sensory feedback and balance, strengthening foot and lower leg muscles and reducing the risk of injuries like shin splints and plantar fasciitis. Individuals with specific foot conditions or biomechanical issues should consult a healthcare professional before making the switch. Transitioning from shoes with thick soles and arch support to completely flat footwear was challenging for me, at first. However, within a few weeks, I noticed improvements in my balance, posture, and the engagement of a wider group of muscles.

And if you fear to look ridiculous with those five toe pouch shoes of years ago—fear not, these days there are plenty of 'barefoot' shoes (minimally padded with soles 2 to 5 millimeters thick) and 'zero drop' (having no height differential between the heel and forefoot) options that look perfectly 'normal' and don't require you to cocoon each toe in a pouch of its own—though you can certainly make a visible statement about your passion for foot health by slipping into a pair of 'five fingers' shoes.

In addition to footwear, clothing played a significant role in my comfort and mobility. Gradually, I began to only purchase and wear clothes that allowed a full range of motion, making movements like sitting on the floor easier and encouraging me to stretch spontaneously—whenever my body was asking for it—before my postural discomfort turned into pain. I noticed an improvement not only in physical comfort but also in my overall mood throughout the day.

Breathability is another factor, benefitting skin and body temperature. As you make this transition to more comfortable and natural clothing and footwear, you'll notice an increase in body awareness—proprioception—as well as a sense of groundedness and ease.

Breath, Body, and Wearable Technology

As I continued to incorporate practices for deeper body awareness, I found myself captivated by somatic breath and bodywork. The effects these practices had on me and my clients were striking, often creating an instant sense of liberation and control, reducing feelings of victimhood and replacing them with a tangible sense of agency and bodily autonomy. This set me on a path of discovery ranging from the arena of modern functional movement practices (multi-joint actions we perform daily, like tying shoes or standing, based on real-world situations) to realms beyond like Ashtanga Yoga, Pranayama Breathwork, Kundalini Meditation, autogenic training, progressive muscle relaxation and Yoga Nidra.

This path of discovery blossomed into a heartfelt passion for teaching these practices.

My clients—ranging from professional athletes seeking peak performance to individuals recovering from trauma and executives aiming for optimal mental agility—have impacted me deeply. They are people from all walks of life, people of every sort of suffering and limitation, and of every sort of aim—yet everywhere I am amazed at the resilience of the human spirit, the tenacity of hope, and our ability to overcome. Perhaps there is some unchanging seed of identity deep inside us; but when it comes to suffering and joy, and finding purpose, I am utterly convinced of our ability to create a better life.

Many of my clients, after just a few sessions, shared that they would have prioritized self-care much more proactively if they had understood the value of holistic wellness—or (less forgivable) if it didn't require an excessive, ongoing daily commitment. I get that. Change is tough, particularly when life is already complex and full of responsibilities. We prefer simple, natural approaches that fit our current lifestyle. A balance must be sought, a balance between the relentless pursuit of peak performance and the vital need to luxuriate in the tranquility of rest. This balance isn't universal; it's a personal equation tailored to each individual's current circumstances, yearnings, and inherent needs.

I've helped many clients find simple ways to incorporate breathing and body awareness exercises into their daily life and work. This not only helps with general physical and mental posture, but also in specific instances of need: preparing for a long-haul flight, or a conference or athletic events. The results were impressive. Even my athletic clients who had previously won Olympic medals experienced noticeable improvements in their comfort and performance. The key realization was that their mental toughness was significantly enhanced when their body and mind were at ease. We can train our bodies to the limit, but it's only sustainable when we cultivate the focus and natural movement in the general landscape of our lives.

Some of the universally helpful breathing exercises I advocate include Diaphragmatic Breathing, Box Breathing, and the 4-7-8 Breathing Technique, described below:

- **Diaphragmatic Breathing:** By emphasizing engagement of the diaphragm, this technique promotes deeper, oxygen-rich inhalations. This method of breathing enhances oxygen exchange and activates the parasympathetic nervous system, leading to relaxation and reduced stress.

- **Box Breathing:** This rhythm-based technique, often utilized by high-pressure professionals, involves inhaling for four counts, holding for four, exhaling for four, and then holding again for four. This focused cycle helps divert the mind from stressors, fostering calmness and enhancing mental clarity.

- **4-7-8 Breathing:** Conceived by Harvard-trained medical doctor and founder of the Arizona Center for Integrative Medicine, Dr. Andrew Weil, this technique offers a method for deep relaxation. Many employ this counting technique to manage stress and anxiety through controlled breathing. Specifically, it involves inhaling for the count of four, holding one's breath for the count of seven, and exhaling for the count of eight.

With their diverse and particular benefits, some combination of techniques like these caters to the differing needs of each client. It's worth noting that there are additional techniques I am familiar with, but I typically don't recommend them unless deemed necessary based on specific circumstances.

The next phase of transformation involves integrating technology into the process. We use tools to measure changes in postural alignment and physical performance, my clients could now not only feel the difference but also see the tangible results for themselves.

Using innovative technologies like postural analysis, we are able to map the shifts in postural alignment before and after the switch to more ergonomic clothing and footwear. The visuals provided by these apps enable clients to see in real-time how their posture improves as they move away from constrictive outfits and more fully inhabited their body and breath. Some opt to embed new habits in daily life through wearable devices like posture notifiers and breathing trackers. These devices can, respectively, alert the wearer when they compromise their ideal posture by slumping or bending improperly, and help track breathing rate and quality, making it easier to develop consistent mindful body and breath awareness.

As wearable fitness trackers become more commonplace, it's easy to quantifiably demonstrate how simple changes can optimize performance. These devices measure and record a variety of parameters including heart rate, heart rate variability (HRV), blood oxygen level (SpO2), body temperature, skin conductance, steps taken, and estimated calories burned. As clients adjusted their clothing selections and focused on increasing their proprioception, many found that they could walk or run longer distances, their average heart rate decreased, and they experienced increased overall stamina and endurance.

The application of technology in this context didn't just provide hard data, it played a crucial role in fostering a sense of accomplishment and motivation among my clients. The visualization of their progress over time, represented in graphs and charts, bolstered their determination to continue their journey toward improved physical health and well-being. Technology has also made it easier to customize and fine-tune each client's journey based on their body type, fitness level, and health goals to maximize their results.

HOLIS**TECH**

My clients have experienced great success with this multi-dimensional strategy that blends comfortable attire with techniques to increase body and breath awareness. This comprehensive approach caters to both the mind and body, promoting measurable improvements in physical performance while also providing a sense of ease and mental clarity.

Mind-Body Connection: The Influence of Trauma

As mentioned, my childhood was not easy. My family and I were derided as infidels and frequently harassed for our beliefs.

I didn't immediately associate these experiences with trauma, however. My culture wasn't one that recognized such things. Terms like 'self-care' and 'holistic' were unheard of. I overlooked the physiological changes occurring within myself and my loved ones during those years. It was only later that I realized how unprocessed trauma could manifest both physically and mentally, often lingering for years without being acknowledged.

When I first broach the subject of the mind-body connection with my clients, emphasizing that we all undergo some form of healing—whether acknowledged or not—I am often met with confusion and denial. However, drawing from the rich historical context of this connection, and highlighting the tangible physical impacts of mental states, the skepticism began to wane.

I pointed out the psychosomatic responses they might have experienced, like how anxiety can manifest as a real stomach ache or how chronic stress might have led to hypertension. By tapping into the neurobiological links, I demonstrated how the brain's perception of experiences, especially traumatic ones, sends signals throughout the body, affecting their overall health and well-being.

The placebo effect serves as a powerful example. If our belief in a mere sugar pill can bring about actual health improvements, it speaks volumes about the two-way connection between our mind and body.

I also often touch upon the significance of mindfulness, which has startling healing properties. Many clients find motivation in knowing that practices like meditation and breathwork aren't just about mental peace, but have tangible benefits for physical health.

The real breakthrough however, often comes when I delve deeper into trauma—especially childhood experience. Even if long forgotten, childhood experiences can have an impact which ripples. They started recognizing their past or current experiences fitting within this definition, realizing that the lingering effects of trauma could be traced back to the intricate interplay between their mind and body.

This is often difficult to come to terms with. It requires a long period of self-analysis, even deconstruction or 'undoing' in some way. As time goes on though, they begin to understand and identify with the idea more deeply, the initial confusion and denial transformed into acceptance and a keen interest in holistic approaches to their well-being.

To further illuminate the concept and its implications, I presented them with a definition and symptom list compiled by a group of mental health experts. Here is what I shared with them:

> "Trauma is an overwhelming experience or a series of such experiences that go beyond an individual's coping capacity, destabilizing their sense of safety, well-being, and perception of the world. It can arise from various incidents, like accidents, natural disasters, violence, abuse, or significant emotional or psychological stressors. These experiences can leave lasting imprints on a person's physical, mental, and emotional health.
>
> The physical symptoms of trauma may manifest as sleep disturbances, fatigue, chronic pain, or changes in appetite and weight. Mental and emotional symptoms can include flashbacks, avoidance and withdrawal, hypervigilance, anxiety, depression, emotional dysregulation, and dissociation. The intensity and duration of these symptoms depend on the individual and the nature of the trauma. It is crucial to note that trauma's effects vary from person to person, and not everyone exhibits the same symptoms. Those impacted by trauma can find healing and learn coping strategies by seeking help from mental health professionals experienced in dealing with trauma."

As my clients and I explore the physical and mental symptoms in depth, everything starts falling into place. It's as if an unseen thread links their past experiences to their present difficulties. Many of us either ignore, suppress, or struggle with these issues for years without fully resolving them. Consequently, we often find ourselves stuck in a cycle of attempting to diagnose or treat the symptoms rather than addressing the root cause. This leads us back to temporary, band-aid solutions again and again.

Attaining optimal physical and mental health is more than simply addressing immediate symptoms. It involves understanding the mind-body connection, acknowledging trauma, and adopting holistic approaches that consider the person as a whole. By prioritizing self-care, exploring personalized treatment options, and incorporating complementary therapies, my clients begin to sustain genuine healing and well-being in our demanding and evolving world.

For many of my clients, unlocking the state of flourishing and peak performance is like cracking a code with three essential keys: physical health, mental well-being, and emotional balance. It's a transformative journey that requires time, effort, and a deep understanding of their unique circumstances. Comprehensive healing unfolds across multiple dimensions, at the intersection of mind and body and emotions.

Biohacking

Venturing into my early 30s, I was introduced to the concept of 'biohacking.' This is the suggestion that, put simply, we can control our bodies and brains to optimize our health, performance, and longevity. It was here that I encountered the works of David Asprey, a pioneer in the field. Known for his Bulletproof diet and his quest for reaching his 180th birthday, Asprey's philosophy of 'biohacking' posits that individuals can use science and self-experimentation to take control of their environment, their biology, and subsequently their health and well-being.

Asprey's ideas had a profound impact on me, opening my eyes to the ways I could manipulate my physiology and cognition to achieve better health. Inspired by his insights, I immersed myself in exploring the research and experimenting with various techniques. It led to the discovery of another layer of healing that I hadn't realized existed: that our health is not a passive state but something that we can actively shape.

One of the key components of biohacking is 'biostacking,' a concept that involves layering multiple health strategies to achieve synergistic effects. Biostacking strategies can include anything from dietary changes, sleep optimization, and exercise regimens to the use of supplements, wearable tech, or nootropics—substances that claim to improve cognitive function, particularly executive functions like memory, creativity, and focus).

Fascinated, I started a range of different biostacks, including (but not limited to) light therapy, cold exposure, fasting, and nutritional supplementation. Almost immediately I noted improvements in my energy levels, mental clarity, emotional well-being, and overall vitality. It was a revelation. The capacity for self-improvement and self-healing that biohacking offered was nothing short of remarkable.

As I began to weave the principles of biohacking and biostacking into my consulting framework, I observed a clear enhancement in my clients' performance. The changes went beyond simple symptom control. People weren't just surmounting their physical and mental health obstacles—they were flourishing.

This revolutionized how I view trauma and the mind-body connection. It became clear that trauma is not just an emotional or psychological issue, but a holistic one that encompasses our entire being—mind, body, and emotions. This understanding allowed me to offer my clients a more comprehensive, personalized approach to healing, one that recognized their unique biology and empowered them to take an active role in their recovery.

This multi-dimensional journey, steeped in biohacking and biostacking principles, helped in fostering a culture of care and well-being. It challenged conventional paradigms, providing an amalgamation of technology, traditional medicine, mental health support, mentorship, and coaching that was as unique as the individual at its heart.

Diving deeper into the realm of biohacking, I began to explore theories from adjacent fields that seemed to echo and complement the biohacking ethos. Notable among them were the concepts of neuroplasticity, as elucidated by Dr. Norman Doidge, and epigenetics, brought to popular attention by Dr. Bruce Lipton.

Dr. Norman Doidge's revolutionary work in neuroplasticity fundamentally altered our understanding of the brain. He proposed that our brains are not static but malleable, meaning they can change, grow, and adapt throughout our lives. This breakthrough shattered the long-held belief that the brain was a fixed, unchangeable entity. It opened up exciting possibilities for personal development, cognitive performance, and healing. Doidge's assertion that the brain could 'rewire' itself in response to learning, experience, or injury became a foundational pillar in my approach to peak cognitive performance. By incorporating techniques that promote neuroplasticity, such as cognitive-behavioral therapy and mindfulness, my clients and I find ourselves better equipped to address trauma, manage stress, and foster resilience.

Dr. Bruce Lipton's work on epigenetics was another masterpiece. Epigenetics is the study of how our behaviors and environment can cause changes that affect the way our genes work. Lipton's research suggests that our thoughts, behaviors, and environment could influence our genes, turning them 'on' or 'off' and affecting our health outcomes. Lipton's research introduced the concept that we are not merely victims of our genes, but active participants with the ability to influence our genetic expression. This is a somewhat radical departure from the traditional genetic determinism that claimed our genes controlled our destiny in some rigid, fatalistic way. While Lipton's theories have been transformative for many, they remain a point of contention among some scientists. Critics argue that while epigenetics is a real and influential field, the extent to which thoughts and behaviors can alter gene expression might not be as pervasive as Lipton suggests.

Regardless, Lipton's theory was a revelation to me and my clients. We began to see that our daily choices—from our diet, exercise, and sleep habits to our stress management techniques and our mental and emotional states—were not merely influencing our health in the short term, but potentially our genetic expression and long-term health outcomes. In fact, integrating epigenetics into our biohacking toolkit allowed us to better understand and influence our biology, optimizing our performance and development from a truly cellular level.

The concepts of neuroplasticity and epigenetics perfectly dovetail with the ethos of biohacking. They provide a scientific grounding to our belief that we are not passive recipients of our biology but active participants with the capacity to influence our health with holistic and personalized techniques.

HOLIS**TECH**

02
Peak Cognitive Performance

> Focused mind power is one of the strongest forces on earth.

Mark Victor Hansen

There's one childhood certainty about my father that remains imprinted in my mind with crystal clarity: even as a little girl I saw he had a remarkable way with words. He possessed a particular talent for poetry, and I can still recall the magical aura he would create with his verses during our birthdays or on those special occasions.

The beauty and harmony of his words were often met with wide-eyed awe. He was a man who radiated conviction, unabashed. He painted a vivid picture with deftness and elegance–the ideas were complete, yet hinted somehow at truths far deeper. They were fragmented into bite-sized morsels, but each one with many layers of wisdom to discover. They flowed with a unique rhythm that made perfect sense, yet dripped with raw emotions and unspeakable beauty.

Now in his seventies, he continues to astound us with his poetic prowess from time to time, defying the passage of the years and proving that both his creative spirit and cognitive ability remain as vibrant as ever.

As I got older and the skill of reading and writing gracefully found its place in me, I found myself echoing my father's habit. I began to craft my own poetic narratives, trading verses and ideas with my father.

And from this wholesome exchange, there emerged something extraordinary: a heightened state of consciousness. It was as if I was disconnected from the tangible world, yet supremely attuned to some ethereal reality. I found myself submerged in a sea of intense pleasure and happiness—a state of absolute tranquility, yet brimming with energy.

In my naivety, I didn't realize that what I was experiencing had a name in the realm of psychology: this was a 'peak experience.' This is often associated with a 'flow state,' another concept in psychology that denotes a state of immersive engagement, usually triggered by an all-encompassing cognitive performance. Regardless of terminology, this was a profound discovery for me—the realization that the human mind extends beyond temporal, practical affairs such as reading books, memorizing formulas and phrases, or solving problems.

This discovery painted a new perspective for me, a perspective that implied the existence of a deeper, more profound cognitive state that was waiting to be explored.

When I began to explore the realm of mindfulness, I was formally introduced to concepts like sensory deprivation, meditative trance, attention training, and peak cognitive performance. I found I'd been harboring many misconceptions.

For instance, I was under the impression that the purpose of mindfulness was to achieve a state of tranquility or relaxation. While a sense of calm can very well be a byproduct of mindfulness, it is not the primary aim. In my personal experience, my moments of mindfulness were often accompanied by a palpable rush of relaxation, a deep sense of peace that permeated my mind. While it was a comforting illusion to hold on to, it was important for me to understand that mindfulness encompassed more than just achieving a relaxed state or occasional experience of the state of universal oneness and ecstasy (formally known as 'objective samadhi' in traditional meditation practices).

A hesitation that arose quite frequently in my early days—and later with my clients—was the association of mindfulness with spiritual practices and religion. Many were concerned that mindfulness could conflict with their religious beliefs. I would reassure them by explaining that mindfulness, in fact, could enhance their connection with their chosen belief system or higher power. It could help filter out distractions, enabling them to focus on their spiritual path (or their self-discipline if divinity was not part of their worldview).

The roots of mindfulness can indeed be traced back to Hinduism and Buddhism, but all religions, to some degree, incorporate the practice of attention training and meditation. These practices are all geared towards self-improvement and spiritual growth, irrespective of an individual's belief in a higher power. Building on this universal foundation, mindfulness offers us the opportunity to reconnect with ourselves and unleash our highest potential.

Another critical insight I gained from my teachers was that mindfulness was not about altering my thoughts and feelings. It was, instead, a tool to change my relationship with them. Whether these thoughts and feelings were comforting or disturbing, mindfulness was not intended to change them but to help me comprehend the correlation between my awareness and these inner experiences.

I discovered that, while mindfulness is not inherently 'complex' (after all, it's a practice that has been around for thousands of years), it isn't necessarily easy to master. The key to enhancing cognitive ability through mindfulness is consistency, a trait many of us struggle with. It's simpler to allocate two hours once a month than it is to commit to a daily practice of 10 minutes, or even an hourly practice of 30 seconds.

Today, scientific research is not only validating the efficacy of mindfulness practices but also turning this domain into a thriving field of study. One of the most impactful studies in this regard is Jon Kabat-Zinn's research on Mindfulness-Based Stress Reduction (MBSR). He found that participants who engaged in an eight-week MBSR program showed significant reductions in stress levels, improvements in mental well-being, and even demonstrated positive physiological changes such as lowered blood pressure.

In a sense, we could consider our ancestors as the original biohackers. Very different from the skeptic (and the neuroscientist) of today, the ancients looked at reality through a framework of narrative. They looked at nature as a collection of personalities, forces not merely of structure but of intent and even 'spirit.' When they performed their sacred rituals, when they sang or chanted or imbibed their psychedelic substances, they were leveraging the mind-body connection with a powerful and 'embodied' sort of abandon which reveals truth through experience—something the scientific method cannot directly speak to.

The intuitive wisdom of our forefathers, now substantiated by modern scientific evidence, continues to enrich our understanding and application of mindfulness in today's world.

The advent of functional magnetic resonance imaging (fMRI) technology has unlocked an extraordinary window into the inner workings of the mind during meditation.

Renowned researchers, such as Dr. Richard Davidson from the University of Wisconsin-Madison, have conducted in-depth studies involving Tibetan Buddhist monks to explore the effects of meditation on the brain. When the monks entered a meditative state inside an fMRI scanner, there were notable shifts in brain activity. Increased activity was observed in areas such as the prefrontal cortex, associated with attention, emotional regulation, and various other dimensions of well-being.

Decreased activity was noticed in the amygdala, the part of the brain associated with stress and anxiety. This not only demonstrates the immediate impact of meditation on brain function but also suggests the potential for long-term structural changes, corroborated by other studies that have shown increased grey matter density in seasoned meditators. These shifts in brain activity and potential structural changes illustrate the tangible and enduring impact of meditation practices.

The arrival of such technological evolutions and scientific breakthroughs has gifted us a second chance - an opportunity to delve into the depths of mindfulness from a renewed, empirical perspective. These findings were corroborated by my personal practice. Mindfulness is about maintaining complete attention towards moment-to-moment experiences, in an open and nonjudgmental way. As soon as I embraced this, and gave up my search for some momentary sensation of peace or ecstasy, I began to notice a drastic shift in my perspective. I realized that it was relatively easy to keep my full attention on experiences that were enjoyable or interesting, such as reading a favorite book, watching a beloved TV show, or conversing with a close friend. The real challenge lay in maintaining that open and non-judgmental attitude, particularly during less pleasant experiences.

This is a struggle that most of us encounter. The tendency to judge or react to what we perceive can often overshadow the purity of the moment. By training our minds to observe without judgment, we can enhance our understanding of the world around us, and thus also our reaction to it. This unfiltered observation leads to a greater sense of acceptance, peace, and empathy toward ourselves and others.

Perhaps one of the most profound lessons I've learned through mindfulness is that 'we are not our thoughts or feelings.' We often identify so strongly with our internal narratives that we forget they are merely transient elements of our consciousness, not definitive markers of who we are. Mindfulness taught me to step back and observe these narratives without getting caught up in them, providing a greater sense of self-awareness and control. It encouraged me to slow down, pay attention, and engage fully with each moment. It helped me cultivate compassion, patience, and understanding—not just for myself, but also those around me. It was a path toward living more fully, deeply, and authentically.

On a deeper level, practicing mindfulness encouraged me and many of my clients to confront and accept negative thoughts and feelings rather than suppressing or avoiding them. This was a difficult process, but it was ultimately liberating, helping us to break free from harmful patterns of thinking and respond more effectively to life's challenges.

Precognition and Parapsychology: Exploring the Mystery of my Childhood Encounters with Precognitive Dreams

Ever since I was a kid, the realm of dreams has fascinated me—and more specifically, the phenomenon of precognition through lucid and precognitive dreams. I remember periods when I would be swept away by intricate dreams filled with vivid details about individuals grappling with particular mental or physical health challenges. Sometimes, these dreams would evolve into sublime healing experiences, while others took darker turns into brutal nightmares, even foretelling the abrupt end of life for these people.

The subjects of these dreams varied widely. Sometimes they were close family members or friends, at other times complete strangers. What startled me, though, was the uncanny way these dreams often manifested in reality within a short span of time, sometimes within mere hours or days.

There was a distinguishing factor to these dreams. In my standard dreams or nightmares, I was typically quite emotionally involved. I would wake up with a rush of fear or exhilaration, needing a moment to calm and reassure myself that all was well. During these dreams though, I would find myself fully lucid, and wake up feeling incredibly calm, harboring a profound sense that what I had dreamt was undoubtedly going to come to pass.

I won't lie: navigating such experiences as a child was bewildering. Even for my parents, it was tough to fully comprehend. Luckily, they were familiar with Carl Jung's psychology, which allowed them to create a safe space where they could listen to my experiences openly. They reassured me that the manifestation of these dreams in reality was neither my fault nor to my credit. Jung, too, cautiously questioned the nature of these 'meaningful coincidences,' coining the term 'synchronicity.' He situated precognitive dreams within his broader theories about the nature of the unconscious mind (into which he believed dreams were a window) and its relationship to reality, using the concept of synchronicity as a way to explore the interactions between the conscious mind, the unconscious, and the external world.

My parents' support and understanding of these concepts was invaluable, especially since these dreams occurred a few times a year. We managed these episodes with the guidance of our close family friend, Dr. Modrick, a well-known neuroscientist and brain surgeon. He was the one who introduced me to the intriguing world of human consciousness, and the mysteries of parapsychology.

These early encounters with the otherworldly realm set the stage for a more profound exploration in my teenage years. I yearned to dive deeper, to understand the roots of these experiences. Little did I know, this journey was less about getting to the bottom of it and more about embracing the mystery of what makes us human!

In my teenage years, I began venturing into meditation and breathwork, driven by an innate curiosity about life's mysteries. My fascination led me towards ancient wisdom and esoteric practices, though it was not always a straightforward pursuit. The challenge lay in identifying legitimate practices that weren't blatantly counter-scientific or stigmatized as cults by mainstream society. This scrutiny, however, pushed me to conduct comprehensive research before delving into these practices. Many of them championed the attainment of altered states of consciousness as their primary goal—a concept that was intensely intriguing for me. However, this was counterbalanced by the prohibitive stance of most organized religions towards such pursuits.

For someone who hadn't ever brushed against the uncanny edges of precognition, it might have been easier to overlook these urges. But, for me, the allure was irresistible. I often found myself in the role of an 'edge walker,' carefully exploring the boundaries between the seen and unseen worlds, attempting to draw as close as possible without overstepping.

This was made more challenging by my residence in a country where such practices were forbidden, and where sourcing translated books on the subject was virtually impossible. When I moved to the United States however, the landscape shifted dramatically.

America offered me a broader horizon, where my exploration took a deep dive into the mysteries of consciousness, supernatural experience, and the intriguing field of Human Potential Movement. This exploration dovetailed an era famously dubbed the 'psychedelic 60's', a period characterized by the blooming counterculture that was questioning established norms and awakening to possibilities.

HOLIS**TECH**

"America offered me a broader horizon, where my exploration took a deep dive into the mysteries of consciousness, supernatural experience, and the intriguing field of Human Potential Movement."

The genesis of the Human Potential Movement was embedded in this era of societal change, fueled by a growing disenchantment with traditional power structures. This was a movement pushing against the confines of established norms, propelled by the belief that every individual is a treasure trove of untapped potential.

The movement owes its birth to the tenets of Humanistic Psychology. The pioneers of this perspective, psychologists like Carl Rogers and Abraham Maslow, turned the spotlight on self-actualization, emphasizing the inherent human drive to fulfill potential. They encouraged a focus on love, creativity, and self-esteem as central to human existence. They introduced the idea of 'peak experiences', those moments of profound joy and euphoria—as pivotal to comprehending human motivation.

Amid the throbbing heartbeat of the counterculture era, the Human Potential Movement found fertile ground to grow.

While these movements were borne out of different circumstances, they shared an underpinning theme: a pursuit to explore, understand, and expand the boundaries of human consciousness. As I delved deeper, I began to feel these weren't merely historical movements or isolated phenomena. They were part of a broader tapestry of human evolution, part of our eternal quest for self-understanding. And it was a journey I was excited to continue.

My passion for parapsychology has grown steadily over the years, fueled not only by my own experiences but also stories and conversations with others. While working with individuals facing terminal illnesses, I've been privy to stories of near-death experiences that range from breathtakingly beautiful to heart-wrenchingly terrifying. Some share visions of serene landscapes and reunions with loved ones, while others recount harrowing tales of accidental overdoses and a glimpse into the abyss.

Then there's the route through psychedelic ceremonies, using substances like Psilocybin, LSD, and DMT. These stories, both wondrous and daunting, have further convinced me of the vast complexity of our consciousness.

In my quest to understand these phenomena however, I've made a conscious choice: to stand as an observer, neither endorsing nor condemning these experiences and practices. My goal is to capture and convey these insights, allowing them to shed authentic light on the spectrum of human consciousness without the coloration of personal judgment.

I must admit that some of my experiences have taken on a deeply personal dimension, intertwining with my life and those of my loved ones in ways that mystify and intimidate me. An example: my fascination with the Titanic, and my aversion to water transportation. It's always been there, and seems simply inexplicable. Though I'm not an active believer in past lives, as a teenager I would often joke about having drowned on the Titanic in some past life.

When I met my now-husband, Benjamin, I was astounded to discover that he too (despite his passion for travel and exploration) harbored a similar aversion to water transport, and a fascination with the Titanic.

The coincidences didn't stop there. I was rendered nearly speechless when I found out that as a young boy, his father used to call him "Isidor" in affection.

For those acquainted with the history of the Titanic, the names Isidor and Ida Straus might ring a bell. Ida and Isidor Straus were a wealthy couple who were passengers on the Titanic. They were deeply in love and famously chose to stay together when the ship was sinking, refusing to be separated. Isidor even offered his seat on a lifeboat to another passenger, saying, "I will not be separated from my wife." Tragically, they both perished in the sinking of the Titanic, but their love and sacrifice became a symbol of devotion and marital commitment in the face of disaster. Now, as Aida and Benjamin, I often find myself wondering: could we, in some unfathomable twist of fate, be echoing the experiences of Isidor and Ida? It's a question that lingers and perhaps, will always remain unanswered. Yet, it underscores the mystery and depth of our consciousness, connections, and the very fabric of our existence.

Another curious incident occurred when, on an ordinary morning, I received an unexpected email from Terje G. Simonsen. With no prior connection to him, I learned he was a Norwegian historian and the author of what I'd soon consider a groundbreaking work, "A Short History of (Nearly) Everything Paranormal: Our Secret Powers Telepathy, Clairvoyance & Precognition."

How he came to know about my passion and work in this field remains a mystery to me. Perhaps, in a twist of irony, some precognitive force drew our minds together. Terje invited me to review his work, an offer I gladly accepted. The book proved to be one of the most comprehensive and captivating surveys of the paranormal I'd ever encountered.

Diving into his book, I was transported into a vivid mosaic of the paranormal universe, where forgotten myths met scientific evidence, and testimonials ranged from noted scientists to famed celebrities. Simonsen's narrative compellingly explored the tantalizing idea that these paranormal events might be more than just figments of imagination. With its meticulous research paired with spellbinding storytelling, his book became a beacon in the vast sea of understanding human consciousness and the mysteries it holds.

Was this some mysterious cosmic alignment or just serendipity? Either way, it blossomed into not only a treasured resource but also a cherished bond of friendship for years to come.

Throughout my exploration into parapsychology's captivating depths, I stumbled upon yet another fascinating gem: the Institute of Noetic Sciences (IONS). This is an institute which emanated from the profound cosmic revelation of Apollo 14 astronaut Dr. Edgar Mitchell in 1973. Picture this: Dr. Mitchell, amidst the vast expanse of space, feels an undeniable pull towards a deeper understanding of both science and the inner human spirit, leading to IONS' inception. Here, the words of Dr. Mitchell bring forth the essence of his transcendental journey:

"The experience in space was so powerful that when I got back to Earth I started digging into various literature to try to understand what had happened. I found nothing in science literature but eventually discovered it in the Sanskrit of ancient India. The descriptions of samadhi, Savikalpa samadhi, were exactly what I felt: it is described as seeing things in their separateness, but experiencing them viscerally as a unity, as oneness, accompanied by ecstasy."

The realm of parapsychology is often met with raised brows across a considerable chunk of the global scientific community. The criticism, of course, is the challenge inherent to measuring intangible phenomena; and the undeniable ethical constraint. After all, we can't induce near-death experiences for the sake of research. IONS is one organization navigating this maze. Instead of sidestepping these issues, they embrace the challenge, determined to bridge the yawning gap between science and the mysteries that remain just out of reach.

IONS' mission stirred something deep within me. Their pursuit is not just about academic rigor—it's a quest to unravel the web of our interconnected reality, harmonizing the tangible and intangible, merging scientific scrutiny with personal epiphanies. They are dedicated to methodical research of these esoteric subjects, hosting an assembly of multidisciplinary scientists centered on frontier topics in consciousness.

Among the personalities at IONS is Dr. Dean Radin, their Chief Scientific Officer. His publications, like "Supernormal," "The Noetic Universe," "Real Magic," and "Entangled Mind," represent a convergence of empirical science and profound introspection. He invites readers into a mesmerizing dance between the logical and the ethereal, drawing on his own personal observations drawn from mindfulness, precognition, and other parapsychological' experiences

In early 2023, I delved firsthand into IONS' pioneering research, participating in a study on the potential healing attributes of lucid dreaming. Here was a study daring to ask, "Can lucid dreaming enact tangible changes in our physiology and perhaps even heal?" With PTSD as a focal point, the research weaved EEG recordings during dreams with a deep dive into inflammatory biomarkers before and after these dreams—all juxtaposed against a controlled backdrop. For me, it was more than an experiment—it was a journey, tapping into perhaps the most potent, yet underutilized facet of our being: conscious awareness.

For someone like me, deeply immersed in the realm of parapsychology while earnestly seeking a balanced perspective, IONS represents a necessary bridge. In an era of polarity and stigmatization, IONS seeks to establish a harmonious middle ground.

The Present Moment

When it comes to improving cognitive performance, we cannot undermine the significance of living in the present moment. As an amusing observation, I often suggest to my clients that we might as well add the title of "Professional Time Traveler" to our resumes, for it's not entirely untrue. Our minds journey perpetually between the past and future, seldom anchoring in the present. The landscape or direction of this mental travel varies greatly among individuals, depending on age, stage of life, and circumstance.

My younger clients (those in their teens or early twenties) are typically less burdened with past experience. The future dominates their thoughts, brimming with aspiration and unsettled possibility. Such foresight (when combined with discipline and planning, certainly) possesses an inherent beauty and power The issue, however, arises when this preoccupation with the future turns into excessive fear and anxiety, detaching them from the vital link between their past and their ongoing actions, which form the foundation of any future we envision.

Contrarily, my interactions with clients in their sixties and seventies often reveals a different story. Conversations with them revolve around the past, tinted with the hues of nostalgia, with memories both pleasant and painful, integral to the narrative they spin about their lives. They scarcely broach the topic of the future. There's a unique beauty and power in this retrospective outlook, too, allowing them to learn from past successes and mistakes. It can lead them to neglect, however, their present. Some stop planning for the future, and slide into aimlessness or depression.

When I began practicing mindfulness, I had little awareness of the extent to which these ancient practices intersect with psychology and neuroscience. I remember being baffled when my meditation master first explained that my perceived reality was merely a distorted fraction of the actual reality. This idea, which seemed esoteric at the time, took on a whole new meaning when I later studied 'cognitive distortions' in psychology. Our perceptions often diverge from actual truth, distorting our decision-making process.

Diving into the depths of mindfulness, I found myself unexpectedly resonating with the profound tenets of psychology, particularly through the lens of Gestalt therapy. This wasn't merely a therapeutic practice; it was akin to a transformative odyssey, passionately magnifying one's self-awareness, cultivating a deep sense of autonomy, and charting a course toward intentional living. While numerous therapies delve into the shadows of one's history, Gestalt shimmers uniquely, grounding its core in the pulsating heartbeat of the present.

But what truly fascinated me was Gestalt's foundational belief: that we are continuously and profoundly shaped by our immediate surroundings and experiences. This isn't about passive existence, but active participation. Gestalt therapy posits that when we immerse ourselves completely, heart and soul, in the present moment—when we truly see, feel, and respond to our here and now—we unlock a path to clearer, more genuine self-understanding. And in doing so, we begin to perceive the world, not through a distorted lens, but with fresh, unbiased eyes. It's a revelation that brings the full range of our life experiences into focus, from the nuanced patterns to the broad strokes.

Between the heart of Gestalt therapy and the wisdom of traditional meditation practices lies a common thread: the transformative power of self-awareness. Both paradigms, though hailing from distinct realms, converge on one profound revelation: by actively engaging with our present, we cultivate a pearl of intrinsic wisdom. This newfound awareness not only reshapes our perceptions but also offers us tools to navigate the ever-shifting landscapes of our thoughts and emotions. Meditative practices and therapeutic techniques become complementary instruments, each shedding light on the other, providing a holistic perspective on self-discovery and healing.

Nowadays, I deeply appreciate the wisdom of my meditation teacher who introduced me to many of these in-depth mindfulness meditation practices, including cognitive defusion, a technique that teaches you to separate yourself from your thoughts and feelings. It's often practiced by mentally stepping back and observing your thoughts as if they are leaves floating down a stream, or clouds passing in the sky. The aim is not to change or judge the thoughts, but to simply notice them and let them pass. As someone who is naturally introspective, I initially found this challenging. With consistent practice however, I learned to view my thoughts and feelings as transient events in my consciousness, rather than as absolute truths, or defining aspects of myself. This practice has been particularly effective in helping me disentangle from unhelpful thoughts and feelings, especially those related to past traumas.

In my clinical work I have seen that, subconsciously, a staggering number of us over-identify with our traumas and past mistakes. When a therapist or counselor attempts to help us process and resolve these traumas, we often feel affronted by the idea of letting go. These experiences have become an integral part of our self-concept. Through mindfulness and meditation though, we learned to reinterpret our experiences, understanding that we are not defined by our traumas or mistakes; instead, we see ourselves as the consciousness that has navigated through these experiences. This new perspective readies us to let go of past pains and stop over-identifying with them.

In our mindfulness sessions, after practicing cognitive defusion, I always encouraged my clients to continue working on this concept with their therapist or counselor. This collaborative approach ensured safe and purposeful navigation through their inner landscapes.

The journey into mindfulness and psychological therapies like Gestalt is nothing short of transformative. Once more, it's through this confluence of ancient practices and modern psychological insights that we find the truth: the key to well-being lies not in the distant past or an uncertain future, but in the present moment.

Growth Mindset vs. Fixed Mindset: Shaping Success through the Power of Belief

As I journeyed alongside my clients, it became increasingly evident to me that the very bedrock of their success (or lack thereof) was usually their deeply ingrained beliefs. These mental structures weren't just guiding their decisions; they were sculpting their life paths by influencing the myriad of choices they made along the way. This realization bore a striking resemblance to a fundamental principle I'd come across in my professional readings—the concepts of fixed and growth mindsets, as described by Dr. Carol Dweck.

Over three decades ago, Dr. Dweck found herself intrigued by students' varied reactions to setbacks. While some students seemed resilient, bouncing back from failure unruffled, others appeared deeply affected by even minor complications. This observation, drawn from a vast pool of student behaviors, culminated in Dweck's coining of the terms 'fixed mindset' and 'growth mindset.'

In essence, these terms shed light on the foundational beliefs individuals harbor about their ability to learn and evolve. Those with a growth mindset are buoyed by the conviction that they can always enhance their intelligence and capabilities. They recognize the potency of their effort as a transformative tool. They're not just inclined to exert more; they believe that this extra mile can actually make a monumental difference. This philosophy naturally propels them to higher levels of achievement.

But here's where it gets fascinating. Recall the idea of neuroplasticity. Modern neuroscience suggests that our brains are dynamic structures, malleable and adaptable. The age-old notion that our brains are rigid, set in their ways past a certain age, has been beautifully debunked. Research shows how, with consistent practice and engagement, our brains forge new neural pathways, strengthen existing bonds, and develop insulation to hasten the flow of neural impulses. So, in many ways, our actions, right from the strategies we employ to the lifestyle choices we make, have a profound impact on our neural growth. This concept aligns perfectly with the essence of a growth mindset: that with the right beliefs and actions, we are constantly evolving, our brains reshaping, and our potentials ever-expanding.

For my clients, understanding and internalizing these principles wasn't just enlightening; it was transformative. Their belief systems, now rooted in a growth mindset, not only fueled their professional trajectories but also paved the way for holistic personal growth.

Many of my clients initially came to me confined by a fixed mindset. They believed their intellectual capacities and talents were static, immutable attributes. This mindset manifested in their lives as an insurmountable barrier to growth. They saw challenge itself as a sign of misguided ambition. Obstacles were not opportunities, a natural part of any landscape; they were signs of inherent inadequacy.

It shouldn't be surprising by now that this limiting perspective hinders growth and resilience, constraining us to our comfort zones, stifling our great potential.

As a client began to embrace a growth mindset however, a remarkable transformation occurred. Intelligence and talents were not set in stone but clay, ready for our molding. With the understanding that they could nurture and develop their abilities, they began to view challenges as opportunities for growth. Failure became a powerful tool for learning, rather than a mark of defeat.

This new sense of direction empowered them to tap into their peak cognitive performance. They realized that their mindset could either be a powerful catalyst or a roadblock in their path to success. By embracing a growth mindset, they significantly reduced their cognitive load, resulting in improved performance in all areas of life.

What truly amazed me was how this growth mindset expanded beyond their personal lives. As they began to strengthen their cognitive abilities, they witnessed an undeniable impact on professional decision-making. Once overwhelmed by decision fatigue, they now stood strong, armed with clarity and confidence. This not only allowed them to make smarter, more effective decisions but also enhanced their overall productivity and efficiency at work.

Yet, as the journey progressed, I observed another peculiar phenomenon. While the growth mindset had largely positive impacts, it also came with a caveat. I noticed some clients succumbing to an 'overextended' growth mindset, pushing themselves relentlessly without considering the potential for burnout. If not held in balance with self-care and rest, a single-minded fixation on self-improvement will lead to exhaustion and stress.

Recognizing this, we worked on finding a balanced approach, embracing the growth mindset while also acknowledging and respecting physical and cognitive limits. The goal was to strive for continuous improvement, but not at the expense of their well-being.

To facilitate this balanced approach and find tangible measurements, we once again turned to the power of technology. By adopting the latest wearable devices like EEG-powered headbands, we could measure brain activity in real time. These headbands, equipped with sensors to detect electrical patterns in the brain, provided real-time feedback on various states of consciousness, from alertness to deep meditation. This allowed our users to differentiate the states of calm and focus from those of a drifting or active mind, offering insights to refine their meditation practice.

To explore their cognitive processes from another angle, we also incorporated fNIRS technology. This is another non-invasive wearable technology that uses near-infrared light to determine areas of the brain with increased blood flow, indicating heightened activity. Through fNIRS, we gained insights into which regions of the brain were more active during different meditation techniques or states. Together, these interventions offered a transparent view into their mental landscapes, bridging ancient meditation practices with the precision of modern neuroscience in real-time.

One client, a high-performing executive, was constantly weighed down by pressure, leading to decision fatigue and anxiety. By using an EEG-enabled mindfulness app, he received instant feedback on his cognitive and emotional state. This technology helped him recognize and manage his stress levels. Insights from the app gave him a clearer understanding of his physical and mental limits, teaching him when to take breaks and rejuvenate rather than simply powering through his fatigue.

A wearable device was similarly transformative for a professional athlete. She was accustomed to the conventional wisdom of pushing her boundaries relentlessly. The device provided physiological data that illustrated the importance of balance and recovery in achieving peak performance. It showed when she was inching towards overtraining, helping her prevent potential injuries and burnout.

In both of these cases, technology has played an instrumental role in shedding light on the often-overlooked nuances of mental and physical well-being. Whether it's an executive grappling with the daily pressures of the corporate world, or an athlete pushing the limits on the field, the ability to access real-time data about one's state of mind and body. This is a truly unprecedented advantage, and paves the way for sustainable peak performance. This is especially pertinent when considering how contemporary demands can sometimes obscure the fine line between healthy exertion and detrimental overexertion.

As we delve deeper into the tangible benefits of using technology to monitor and manage cognitive states, it becomes evident that we're on the cusp of a new era in understanding human brain functionality. To truly appreciate the possibilities, it's crucial to understand the foundational science behind it. Central to this is Electroencephalography, commonly known as EEG. A closer look into EEG reveals the intricate symphony of brainwaves that guide our every thought, emotion, and action.

EEG and Brain Training

Electroencephalography (EEG) offers an insightful window into the workings of the human brain. It measures the direct electrical activity produced by neurons. Each neuron emits a tiny electrical charge, and when they synchronize, these collective impulses form brainwaves. These brainwaves can be categorized based on their frequencies:

- **Gamma Brainwaves (32-100 Hz):** These are the highest frequency waves, often associated with heightened perception, learning, and problem-solving. In fact, seasoned meditators often exhibit a surge in Gamma waves, showcasing their profound focus.
- **Beta Brainwaves (13-32 Hz):** These are dominant during awake, alert states. Whether you're making a decision or solving a complex problem, Beta waves are at the forefront.
- **Alpha Brainwaves (8-13 Hz):** These represent a state of relaxed alertness. When you're meditating or letting your mind wander peacefully, Alpha waves are most prominent.
- **Theta Brainwaves (4-8 Hz):** These are linked to deep relaxation, daydreaming, and even light sleep. They play a pivotal role in learning, healing, and personal growth.
- **Delta Brainwaves (<4 Hz):** These have the lowest frequency and govern the deep, dreamless sleep phase, aiding in the body's recovery and healing.

To harness the power of these waves, EEG neurofeedback training starts with a detailed assessment of one's typical brainwave patterns. Post-assessment, we set specific goals. For example, someone with anxiety might benefit from upregulating Alpha and downregulating Beta waves. Throughout the training sessions, users receive immediate feedback, enabling them to actively and consciously shift their brainwave states. Over multiple sessions, the brain becomes adept at entering these desired states without external input.

As we delved deeper into understanding cognitive processes, we integrated fNIRS technology. This non-invasive wearable tech uses near-infrared light to detect regions of increased brain blood flow, suggesting heightened activity.

fNIRS and Brain Training

Functional near-infrared spectroscopy (fNIRS) measures changes in blood oxygenation, offering a unique perspective on neural activity. By focusing on the prefrontal cortex via sensors placed on the forehead, fNIRS captures the dynamics of a region instrumental in executive functions like planning, decision-making, and behavioral adaptations. Here's how the training typically unfolds:

- **Sensor Placement:** The fNIRS sensors target the prefrontal cortex.
- **Monitoring Blood Flow:** By tracking blood oxygenation in real-time, we get a real-time map of neural activity.
- Feedback Loop: Similar to EEG, individuals receive feedback based on their neural performance. This feedback often takes the form of visual or auditory cues.
- **Brain Strengthening:** With repeated sessions, the brain undergoes neuroplastic changes, solidifying neural pathways associated with enhanced focus, decision-making, and other executive functions.

Taken together, these technological tools have provided a clear and detailed picture of unseeable mental landscapes, effectively integrating ancient meditation wisdom with the precision of modern neuroscience. With these personalized insights, my clients experienced significant shifts in both their personal and professional lives. They went from being constantly overwhelmed by decision fatigue to a state of empowered clarity. Their decision-making abilities improved, their productivity increased, and they became more effective in their roles. These experiences demonstrated how combining the right mindset with advanced technology could provide a path to achieving peak human performance without having to pay the price of testing limits through overexertion and burnout. This serves as a potent reminder that our beliefs can truly shape our journey to success.

Learnings on Self-Transformation from the Metamind Program

The Metamind program is an eight-week, technology-enabled mindfulness course I've been leading, enhancing, and collecting data on for over five years. Participants typically experience significant transformations by the second or third week. Within approximately twenty-one days of diligent practice, most participants exhibited significant changes in their interactions with unwelcome thoughts and feelings. There is a marked shift from distress and doubt towards curiosity and exploration. Participants start acknowledging the complexity of their minds, and recognize the importance of reserving adequate time and space for processing their thoughts and feelings.

Intriguingly, their attention span often improves significantly as they become less agitated by the inherent wandering nature of the mind. They recognize that it is normal for thoughts to drift, and rather than resisting this natural process, they learn to embrace it with grace and patience. A fundamental technique to cultivate is the practice of heightened awareness, where they learn to redirect their attention consciously toward what they genuinely desire to focus on.

As participants become more attuned to their thought patterns and bodily sensations, they grow increasingly forgiving towards their past mistakes. They become less bothered by the need to repeatedly redirect their attention, understanding that it's part of the process. They become less attached to the idea of 'getting it right' every single time. Recognizing that there will be ups and downs, they understand that the main key is consistency. This objective observation of the mind and emotions empowers them to exert control over things within their grasp while simultaneously becoming more accepting of things beyond their control.

What I am describing is known as metacognition—the ability to think about one's thinking. By understanding the patterns of our minds, we can start recognizing and then consciously reshaping these patterns.

The next step of course is learning to sustain this mindset consistently across time, ensuring a sustainable improvement in cognitive well-being, rather than just transient results or a 'honeymoon effect'.

HOLISTECH

The idea is not merely to experience mindfulness in an individual session, but to integrate it as an essential component of our lifestyle, to have it as a tool whenever we need to recalibrate our emotional and mental state.

This requires us to dive deeper into the diverse range of techniques, exploring the nuances of their personal effectiveness. I analyze a client's physical and mental health history, biofeedback data, and even the set and setting in which they are conducting their practices, all to better understand what works best for them as an individual.

Suppose their heart rate was lowered, inducing calm. Was it the breathing techniques? Was it the body scan practice, enhancing physical awareness and making them more emotionally attuned? By dissecting these elements, we hope to design a personalized routine they can employ to achieve consistent results.

To reinforce these practices and ensure their sustainability, we also work on building mental resilience. Just like physical muscles, the mind too needs to be trained consistently to strengthen its ability to recover from distractions or stress, adapt to change, and maintain focused attention. This is done through consistent mindfulness practices coupled with exercises aimed at enhancing mental flexibility and fostering a growth mindset.

At some point along the journey, it always becomes crucial to integrate mindfulness practices into daily routines. I like to help my clients gradually shift their emphasis from relying on my guidance during sessions toward becoming self-reliant. I encourage my clients to develop a sense of ownership over improving their own mental and physical well-being.

I introduce them to various techniques that could be easily incorporated into their everyday lives, such as mini-meditation sessions during their lunch breaks, mindful breathing while stuck in traffic, or a brief body scan before bedtime. The aim is to illustrate that these practices do not necessarily require a dedicated slot of time but can be seamlessly blended into their schedules, a comforting constant amidst the flux of their routines.

The outcome is a program that enables my clients to harness these techniques in their everyday life, be it in the face of a challenging situation at work, a period of personal stress, or simply to find an oasis of calm in the chaos of their day.

To ensure the sustainability of the results, we also work on goal-setting. Each client is encouraged to set small, achievable targets for themselves. These could be as simple as staying mindful during a particular task, maintaining calm in a stressful situation, or simply remembering to take a few mindful breaths during the day. Some clients take it to the next level by devising plans for measured improvement in situations that demand their highest performance. Achieving these goals, small or large, serves as a motivation and a reinforcement of their ability to bring about positive and identity-building change.

Of course, we continue to use technology to track their progress and tweak their individual programs. Wearable technology and apps become trusted companions, providing real-time feedback and guiding them to adjust their techniques as needed. This ongoing monitoring offers them a clear picture of their journey and confidence that they are on the right path. This technological fusion breathes new life into ancient wisdom, enriching it with the precision of instant data and sophisticated analytics.

As my clients continue to regularly practice these techniques, they often notice significant changes. They report increased focus, lower stress, and an overall enhanced ability to deal with life's challenges. In the end, these practices transition from being just therapeutic tools to becoming a way of life. They serve as a compass guiding my clients through the ups and downs of life, a resilient coping skill that they can rely on at any time. This transformation is not just about improving their mental health, but also about enabling them to live more fully, mindfully, and authentically. It is always a privilege to guide them on this journey and to witness their growth and empowerment.

When my clients first come to me, they are often in a state of vulnerability. Overwhelmed and burned out, they face decision fatigue both in their professional and personal lives. But everything changes when they embrace these techniques alongside wearable meditation tracking devices and their corresponding apps. These innovative devices take mindfulness practices, often seen as esoteric and unattainable without years of training, and turn them into something tangible and measurable in real-time. With these tools, my clients gain a clear view of their cognitive functioning and its connection to overall well-being.

HOLIS**TECH**

Metacognition in Daily Life

In the hustle and bustle of modern life, our cognitive states are in constant fluctuation. It's vital to identify and handle these shifts with patience but intentionality. The testimonies of Metamind participants echo the significance of discerning and proficiently managing these cognitive shifts. The feedback I've collected reveals that individuals involved in the program often experience a transformative shift in their interaction with their mental states, intrusive thoughts, and emotions by the second or third week.

On average, participants in the Metamind Program experience an enhancement in their mental efficiency, emotional stability, stress levels, and creativity. But before someone can achieve these states, it's essential for them to know where they're starting from today and be able to communicate it. This may seem counterintuitive, but it isn't always easy to know what and how we are thinking. Like breathing, thinking can be either a conscious or autonomous process. When it's happening autonomously, it's difficult to understand and influence. This is where the concept of metacognition comes into play.

Metacognition refers to the ability to observe, understand, analyze, regulate and reflect upon one's own cognitive processes and emotions. In simple terms, it's about being able to understand and change the way we are thinking, applying different thinking strategies to better deal with different situations.

I began exploring the concept of metacognition during my in-depth study of the impact of mindfulness meditation on behavioral patterns. I discovered that more often than not, we operate on autopilot in our daily activities, unconscious patterns overshadowing deliberate thought and action. This is a result of the ingrained patterns within our mind, which inhibit mindful response—a phenomenon known as automaticity.

Automaticity governs behaviors executed without conscious awareness. Consider driving. The subtleties of changing gears and steering often go unnoticed by experienced drivers. For a fun example, imagine a steering wheel in your hand and try miming the act of merging from the right lane to the left, as if preparing to pass another car. When trying consciously to replicate this normally unconscious act, many people will turn the imaginary wheel from the center to the left and then back to the center, ending the maneuver here and thereby leading their imaginary car directly off the left shoulder of the road. In reality, one must first countercorrect, reversing the change in momentum and bringing the car back in a stable line.

Some researchers postulate that up to 90% of our actions are automatic, emerging through long practice until they no longer need conscious intervention. These patterns extend beyond tangible actions, also affecting our thought processes and emotional responses—including those to stress and setback.

Although automaticity is advantageous in certain scenarios, it can pose significant challenges, especially when change is imperative. Adjusting these automatic patterns in an intentional way requires skill in metacognition.

When one engages in metacognition, they experience a shift from a mode of automatic analysis and response (such as an engineer's tendency to look at a problem from a strictly logical perspective) to a more contemplative or reflective observation of their own mental state and strategy. Instead of just thinking about the problem, with metacognition we allow our perspective to ascend to the 'meta' level where we can choose to think about how we're thinking about the problem, scrutinizing the accuracy and efficacy of our thoughts and thinking strategies.

Gaining skill in metacognition facilitates enhanced comprehension of cognitive and emotional experiences, refined learning, improved problem-solving, more balanced emotional response, and elevated self-awareness. Albert Einstein once said, "You cannot solve a problem with the same mind that created it." Metacognition exemplifies this principle, allowing someone to change their mindset and view challenges with a new perspective.

As an example to illustrate what it means to employ different metacognitive lenses, consider a challenging situation, perhaps a personal goal that seems unattainable. The thought arises, "I can't do this."

First let's consider the way the mind may handle this thought without any metacognitive awareness. In this mental strategy, you may simply interpret this thought as an unquestionable fact and subsequently abandon the endeavor entirely.

Next, imagine applying the metacognitive strategy of observing the thought. In this instance, observing may mean you simply acknowledge the thought's existence without judgment or exploration, like noticing a leaf floating down a stream. You don't dissect the thought or allow it to influence your emotions or actions; you merely recognize it and let it pass, leaving your mind unburdened to approach the situation anew. In this case you are now free to embody Einstein's sentiment.

Finally, we'll consider employing an analytical approach to our metacognition. Remember, this is not analyzing the problem itself, but analyzing your reaction "I can't do this" to assess its roots and validity. You might question why you feel you can't attain the goal or what aspects seem particularly daunting. You then explore whether the thought was a reflection of reality or a manifestation of fear or insecurity, and then use this knowledge to consider how to address the thought constructively. This deeper exploration and reframing can transform the mindset that produced the thought in the first place, aligning with Einstein's principle. You cannot solve a problem with the same mind that created it.

The metacognition phenomenon predominantly operates within the anterior prefrontal cortex of the brain, a crucial area for planning, decision-making, and moderating social behavior. supported by intricate neural networks, each responsible for different aspects of metacognition such as self-reflection and self-monitoring.

The growth of metacognitive capabilities is a gradual process, starting in childhood and continuing through adolescence, intertwined with the development of the frontal lobes and shaped by various genetic, environmental, educational, and socio-economic influences.

To understand the level of an individual's metacognition, tools like the Metacognitive Awareness Inventory (MAI) can be employed. The MAI asks the participant to self-report a true or false answer to statements such as "I ask myself if I have considered all options when solving a problem" and "I am a good judge of how well I understand something." Other techniques seek to identify the gap between a person's confidence on a task and their actual performance. Metacognition-based interventional strategies are commonly used in education, as enhanced metacognition has been directly correlated with improved learning outcomes, heightened problem-solving abilities, and the development of expertise.

Metacognition also plays a crucial role in emotional regulation and is particularly therapeutic for mental health conditions like anxiety and depression, which are characterized by distorted thinking patterns. Metacognitive therapies, a subset of cognitive-behavioral therapies which focus on modifying metacognitive beliefs and strategies, have proven effective in reducing symptoms of various psychological disorders.

Substantiated by rigorous scientific research, metacognition is integral for learning, problem-solving, emotional regulation, and mental health, allowing individuals to move beyond immediate cognition and emotion to a reflective and analytical stance, fostering the cultivation of self-awareness and adaptive learning strategies, leading to improved cognitive and emotional functioning.

Developing a fundamental grasp of metacognition paves the way to the crucial phase of the Metamind program: cultivating mental flexibility. Mental flexibility or cognitive agility pertains to the capability to effortlessly transition between diverse cognitive states as needed, representing superior adaptability in thought processes. After the establishment of metacognitive awareness, the emphasis can shift to the development of mental flexibility, enabling individuals to modify their cognitive states and approaches adeptly to align with differing circumstances.

Progressing to this stage engenders a conducive atmosphere for advanced learning and the resolution of problems and also empowers individuals with enhanced strategic adaptability and cognitive versatility. This enhanced adaptability is especially valuable because it gives us the opportunity to strategically switch between the three most helpful cognitive states: the state of peak cognitive performance, the flow state, and the meditative state. Described below, these states can significantly influence our everyday activities, improving outcomes when employed at the appropriate moment. Unfortunately, many of us are trapped in automaticity, reacting automatically with the state we use most frequently to deal with the type of situation we are facing. If we're lucky, we've developed a tendency to unconsciously utilize one of the three helpful cognitive states, though perhaps not the most ideal of the three for the nuances of the situation at hand. Conversely, the reaction that automatically presents itself could just as likely represent a state of anxiety, rumination, confusion, or panic.

Next we'll explore the three most helpful cognitive states to underscore the desirability of being able to both access them and switch between them on demand.

State of Peak Cognitive Performance

Peak Cognitive Performance is, essentially, when your brain is 'firing on all cylinders'—making decisions, solving problems, and absorbing new information with maximal efficiency. Examples include:

- **Decision Making:** Choosing the best action after evaluating options in business or personal life.
- **Learning & Studying:** Effectively absorbing, understanding, and retaining new data.
- **Fast Response Scenarios:** Quickly and accurately reacting during emergencies or time-sensitive situations.
- **Public Speaking:** Articulating thoughts, recalling facts, and adapting to audience reactions swiftly.

Flow State

Often referred to as "being in the zone", the flow state is when you're so deeply immersed in an activity that you lose self-consciousness. This leads to optimal performance and creativity. Examples include:

- **Creative Endeavors:** Whether it's a painter losing track of time while creating a masterpiece, a writer being deeply engrossed in constructing a narrative, or a musician effortlessly composing a new tune.
- **Athletic Performance:** Think of a basketball player seamlessly making shot after shot, or a dancer moving gracefully on stage, perfectly in sync with the music.
- **Professional Excellence:** A software developer who's so focused that complex code becomes simple or a chef who's so in the moment that a new recipe feels intuitive.
- **Deep Engagement:** When gamers find themselves so engrossed in a video game that hours feel like minutes; or when a researcher becomes so immersed that they lose all track of time.
- **Collaborative Flow:** Team members working on a project, where ideas are bouncing back and forth effortlessly, and the team achieves more than the sum of its parts.

Meditative State

A tranquil, introspective state of mind, often achieved through practices like meditation or deep relaxation techniques. Examples include:

- **Yoga or Meditation:** Engaging in structured meditation sessions or yoga practices that create a calm and focused mental state.
- **Daydreaming:** Drifting off into thought when looking out a window, when walking in nature, or during any quiet moment in which your thoughts are yours alone. This relaxed, contemplative state is characteristic of alpha waves, and is one of the more difficult to attain in today's digitized, endlessly networking, hyperstimulated world.
- **Listening to Music:** This can happen when the music elicits strong emotions or memories—but it doesn't have to be so individual. The power of music appears to be coded in us very deeply. This can also happen when you're simply engrossed in the flow of notes themselves, drifting free of your own mind, isolated from the world. This facilitates a transition between alpha (relaxed alertness) and theta (deep relaxation) states.
- **Watching TV:** In a passive state, where you are just absorbing content without much analytical thought, your brain can be in the alpha state.
- **Pre-Sleep Moments:** Those moments in between wakefulness and sleeping, right before you drift off are dominated by theta waves.

Life doesn't operate in silos, and neither should our cognitive states. Mastering the art of transitioning between them allows us to face challenges gracefully. Many risk being trapped in one cognitive mode (often chronic stress, nowadays) but by leveraging the power of metacognition—thinking about one's thinking—participants of Metamind have been able to reshape their mental patterns. It's worth noting that the practice demands patience and persistence, but the results are profoundly rewarding.

The vision behind Metamind wasn't merely academic; it's a practical and actionable blueprint, rooted in a solid foundation of peer-reviewed research. I see myself as a facilitator, hoping to bridge the gap between knowledge and its real-world application. My genuine aspiration was to offer individuals tools that might assist them in navigating the intricate pathways of life with mindfulness and resilience.

Many of my clients combat depressive episodes, attention disorders, or even trauma. Through the Metamind program, I've witnessed firsthand the transformative effects of regular practice. Equipped with wearable technology, they gained real-time insights into their cognitive processes, making mindfulness not just an abstract practice but a tangible, measurable skill. Their experiences illuminated the significance of a paradigm shift—a harmonious blend of holistic health and technology, essential for future well-being.

HOLISTECH

03
The Art of Aging Well and the Secrets of Timeless Beauty

> # The longer I live, the more beautiful life becomes.

Frank Lloyd Wright

Another intriguing topic that recurrently piqued my interest—and, unsurprisingly, a top concern among my clients—resided at the intersection of mortality and the perception of aging. This demographic, spanning from professional athletes to executives, including individuals in recovery from trauma or addiction, frequently wrestled with their mortality. They grappled with the notion of aging and the perceived inevitability of losing the strength, beauty, and vigor that characterized their youthful years.

In my explorations of philosophy, I've often been fascinated by the mental models we build about beauty and strength, and how these principles manifest in our daily lives. We often construct self-concepts around our physical attributes and abilities. The allure of looking youthful, muscular, slim, wrinkle-free, or being able to run faster or lift more than others is pervasive—especially in our social media-centric society, where digital impressions often overshadow real-world authenticity. We are driven by images that are carefully curated, rather than genuine reflections of reality.

Why are we so captivated by the concept of immortality? What drives this ceaseless pursuit of perpetual youth and vitality? Is it the fear of the unknown, the inevitability of mortality that compels us to seek ways to slow down the march of time? Perhaps it's our innate desire to leave a lasting impact, to be remembered through history and thus defy the ephemeral nature of life itself.

Countering this impulse are those who encourage aging gracefully, sans artificial enhancement Regardless of the motivations, I harbor no prejudice toward either camp—the advocates of embracing natural beauty and aging gracefully sans artificial enhancement or those who opt to harness the power of modern technology to reverse the hands of time. I've witnessed the potency of both perspectives in my clients' journeys—(which itself poses further questions regarding the mind-body connection. A negative self-image can sow seeds of insecurity, spurring conflicts between our self-perception and physical capabilities.

Sometimes, even the slightest change in physical appearance can create an amplified impact on our mental well-being—and vice versa. I've worked with individuals whose physical and cognitive abilities were compromised due to stress-induced premature aging, substance abuse, injuries, or accidents. Observing them regain their vigor—sometimes with the aid of biotechnology—was genuinely magical. It was awe-inspiring to see someone rise from the depths of depression and anxiety to reclaim significant portions of what they believed they had lost.

On the flip side, of course, I've seen people become obsessed with this process of self-alteration, so intent on achieving their version of perfection that they began to look unnatural to any sane observer.

My experiences with the transformations that occur at the confluence of holistic health and technology—particularly in the realm of anti-aging and beauty products—have led me to advocate for a balanced approach. Modern advancements offer a great opportunity to age more gracefully. Conversely, I also see individuals who have never sought any form of enhancement, yet manage to maintain a youthful, vibrant appearance well into their seventies or even beyond.

HOLISTECH

Modalities and Technologies for Aging Well

Today, there are many fascinating holistic health modalities that can support us in maintaining youthfulness and aging well. I've tried these technologies myself, and do my best to help clients choose those that fit best with their goals and motivations. I'll describe some of the top methods I've found success with:

Light Therapy

Light therapy, also known as phototherapy, has shown immense potential in skin rejuvenation. Certain wavelengths of light in particular have been clinically proven to restoratively interact with the skin:

- **Blue (415nm – in the visible spectrum):** Neutralizes the bacteria that contribute to the redness and inflammation associated with acne.
- **Yellow (570nm – in the visible spectrum):** Stimulates biological pathways, reduces inflammation and redness, and boosts lymphatic flow, promoting anti-aging processes.
- **Red (633nm – in the visible spectrum):** Reduces inflammation and redness while promoting cellular repair and circulation for a more vibrant complexion.
- **Near-infrared (830nm – invisible to the eye):** Targets deeper fibroblast cells, stimulating new collagen and elastin production, resulting in plumper, firmer, and more youthful-looking skin.
- **Near-infrared (1072nm – invisible to the eye):** Triggers a more robust cellular response, offering various anti-aging and skin rejuvenation benefits.

Moreover, the effects of photoaging—skin damage caused by prolonged sun exposure—garner significant attention from the scientific community. From ultraviolet (UV) rays to free radicals, our skin faces daily assaults that contribute to premature aging. Antioxidants like vitamins C and E, along with compounds like retinoids, can help neutralize these harmful agents. By practicing sun protection and integrating products rich in antioxidants, we can mitigate the long-term consequences of photoaging, helping to preserve the skin's youthful appearance and, more importantly, its actual health.

Bioidentical Hormone Therapy

Bioidentical hormone therapy involves hormones that are structurally identical to those naturally produced by the body. These hormones are often derived from plant sources and are meticulously formulated to match an individual's hormonal needs. For instance, bioidentical estrogen, progesterone, and testosterone can be used to address hormonal imbalances that may contribute to weight gain, decreased sexual health, and stamina. It's crucial to note that while bioidentical hormone therapy can offer benefits, it should be undertaken under medical supervision, as personalized treatment plans are necessary to ensure safety and efficacy.

Vitamin IV Therapy

Vitamin IV Therapy is yet another modality that has gained traction recently. By delivering essential vitamins and nutrients directly into the bloodstream, this intravenous method bypasses the digestive system, enabling faster absorption and potentially replenishing deficiencies. While some individuals report immediate revitalizing effects, it's important to approach this therapy with caution. A comprehensive assessment of an individual's nutritional needs should guide the formulation of IV vitamin cocktails to prevent excessive dosing and potential adverse reactions.

Radio Frequency (RF) Skin Tightening

In the realm of non-surgical body sculpting solutions, Radio Frequency (RF) Skin Tightening shows great promise. RF is a form of electrical current that converts to heat energy once introduced into the body. This heat, produced by the RF energy, journeys through both the dermal and subcutaneous layers of the skin, igniting a sequence of physiological responses that lead to transformative outcomes.

Within the subcutaneous layers, the heat generated by RF prompts a series of processes that revolve around natural fat metabolism. It stimulates the release of liquid fat from the fat cells, allowing it to disperse into the extracellular matrix. This mechanism culminates in a noticeable reduction in the circumference of the treated area. This approach offers a non-invasive means of targeting stubborn fat deposits, paving the way for a more sculpted and contoured physique.

In the dermal layer, RF's impact is often equally impressive. The heat emanated by the technology affects the collagen fibers—a pivotal protein responsible for maintaining the cohesion of skin tissue. The heat induces the contraction of these collagen fibers, leading to a tightening effect that results in smoother, more supple skin. Moreover, RF's influence extends to fibroblast metabolism, the cells responsible for producing collagen. This acceleration of fibroblast activity translates to heightened collagen regeneration, thus establishing a foundation for long-term skin tightening and firming effects.

Research is still ongoing to explore the long-term effects of RF exposure. Every day, we encounter small amounts of human-made radiofrequency (RF) radiation through devices like cell phones, TV, and WiFi. RF has been thoroughly researched due to its widespread use, and organizations like the FDA and World Health Organization have classified it as "possibly carcinogenic to humans." Yet, there is no definitive proof that RF exposure raises the risk of cancer in humans, even for those with frequent job-related RF exposure. As such, RF skin tightening treatments are widely considered safe and effective alternatives to more invasive treatments.

Exercise

Through my exploration of various modalities, I've recognized the importance of balanced fitness approaches. No matter the technologies employed, it is difficult to make up for the aging caused by an overly sedentary lifestyle. Learning to exercise better (not just more) has become a central part of my beauty and anti-aging ritual. By understanding the impact of targeted exercises, mindfulness, and proper nutrition, I've discovered that sustainable results go beyond simply spending more time at the gym.

Focusing on quality rather than quantity yields optimal benefits, promoting balanced muscle strength, flexibility, and overall well-being. This can mean being mindful of your posture while exercising, and incorporating targeted therapeutic exercises as necessary to balance your strength. It can also mean being aware of the level of joint impact, and occasionally adjusting according to the messages your body is sending.

As in all things, consistency is vital. Light therapy, for example, requires regular sessions to sustain its benefits. Depending on the specific goals and modalities used, a treatment plan may involve multiple sessions per week initially, followed by maintenance sessions.

As I continue to explore these technical details, I recognize that these are evolving sciences. Technology will continue to change, and I won't ever have all the answers, but my commitment to both experiencing and sharing these findings remains resolute.

In our pursuit of graceful aging, let's continue to embrace a balanced perspective. Our fascination with defying the passage of time reflects our humanity, and a valid desire for fulfilled lives. While the fountain of youth may remain always out of reach, the journey itself does hold valuable rewards: inevitable knowledge, inevitable growth, and (if the journey is made wisely) a deeper appreciation for the beauty that accompanies each stage of life.

Acceptance versus Control

Daily life brings us a variety of experiences, some pleasant and some not so much. We readily accept the pleasant ones: receiving a compliment, engaging in a stimulating conversation, accomplishing an engaging task. These experiences are generally welcomed and embraced, since they are agreeable and contribute to our sense of well-being.

When it comes to less pleasant situations like a disagreement, or mundane or uncomfortable tasks, we exhibit a tendency to resist. This is natural. It's human nature to gravitate towards pleasure and retreat from discomfort.

Interestingly, this resistance extends to inevitable realities such as aging, and changes in our physical and cognitive abilities. As the physical allure of youth recedes and cognitive dexterity is diminished, many people see these changes as unpalatable or even terrifying. They are tied though, inherently, to the nature of existence. They will continue to occur. In the broad sphere of beauty, anti-aging, health, and body aesthetics, I've found that many of my clients grapple with a deeper issue than just the surface concern of wrinkles, physical aging, or weight control. Those are the obvious or superficial layers, sure; but we all know this stretches into the deeper realm of self-acceptance, and the psychological implications of personal transformation.

Two particularly notable examples are those related to facial enhancements and body contouring. The contrast between our ideal and our current state is often overwhelming and disheartening. The future theoretical pleasure of appearing a certain way can only offer so much consolation. Depending on the perceived difficulty of attaining our ideal, we often opt not to pursue it at all but rather topple into an endless cycle of aspiration, frustration, and eventual resistance.

Suppose a client wants to lose weight. They will not achieve their goal immediately. They're going to suffer an ongoing tension then, which their brain tells them can only be resolved by reconciling their current reality with their desired state.

Interestingly, the clients who navigate these challenges most effectively are the ones who practice acceptance while also embracing their aesthetic goals as worthy and desirable. They don't suppress their current reality but take consistent, healthy steps. They understand that change (be it in face, body, or performance) is a process, and that acceptance of the present is a vital part.

In both aging and weight control or body contouring, attempts to control or resist change often leads to intensified distress and other counterproductive outcomes, paradoxically including weight gain or an even more distorted body image.

Those who endeavor to maintain their achieved weight or body shape by overly restrictive measures often feel trapped by the fear of regressing. Their fixation on preserving their current state leaves them apprehensive about the future. Conversely, those who accept that body changes are natural and manageable demonstrate a healthier, more sustainable approach to beauty and body image, pursuing a balanced lifestyle, sometimes augmented with certain, safer procedures.

As I mentioned earlier, there's an understandable impulse to view beauty and anti-aging as solely external, focused on altering the physical appearance without any true underlying benefit. However, as their understanding evolved, they began to recognize that true beauty and aging-well are internal states that require acceptance of our current state and the natural changes we undergo. Whether individuals chose to pursue technological interventions to age well and aesthetically enhance their appearance or opt to embrace their natural state, they were actively practicing acceptance rather than remaining indifferent.

This realization was a significant breakthrough for me because it revealed that those who aimed to age gracefully and maintain their well-being did not disregard the changes they were experiencing. On the contrary, they wholeheartedly embraced and enjoyed the journey. Furthermore, we discussed acceptance not being a mere act of liking or agreeing with physical or mental performance decline but rather an understanding of the current state and a commitment to respond to it consciously.

This process required their willingness to engage with the changes they were experiencing, delving into their feelings about their aging process and the balance between acceptance and control. In this mindset, they were able to take realistic responsibility for how they wanted to look and feel and how they wished to relate to their physical appearance.

To many of my clients, integrating technology and anti-aging was immensely valuable, as they could employ the benefits of the latest scientific advancements. Simultaneously, they were able to cultivate a holistic mindset that embraces self-acceptance, self-understanding, and a deeper exploration of the reasons and purpose behind their needs, desires, and actions. This integration allowed us to have a complete experience without it becoming an obsession or leading to passive resignation in the face of inevitable changes.

During these consultations and in-depth conversations, we would often find ourselves navigating a maze of topics rarely explored. Among these were the unsettling ethical quandaries that loomed over us and the ever-present specter of unconsciously forming unhealthy habits. Our journey into the realm of beauty technologies was akin to a walk on a tightrope. It would be easy to slip into the trap of over-reliance on technology. We discovered that while tech advancements can be enticing, an overemphasis on them could leave one neglecting the vital pursuit of inner growth and acceptance.

On the other side was the ethical crossroads. The use of groundbreaking technology for beauty enhancements didn't merely open a door—it flung wide open a Pandora's box of ethical conundrums. We found ourselves questioning body image standards, scrutinizing informed consent, and confronting the potentially unrealistic beauty ideals these advancements could perpetuate.

HOLISTECH

We then encountered a steep hill—the financial implications. Some high-tech solutions, we found, carried a hefty price tag. Their cost could make them inaccessible for many, potentially widening the chasm between those who could and couldn't afford such practices. Though, as with any technology, the enthusiastic early adopters pay the high price that supports cost-reducing developments that eventually improve availability to others.

At the end of our journey, we arrive at an enlightening conclusion: Today, more than ever before, we can access transformative approaches to enhance beauty and navigate the inevitable processes of aging. By mindfully merging holistic practices with technology and balancing our state of acceptance and control, we can safely enhance our experience of wellness throughout life. This delicate equilibrium ensures that external interventions serve to augment, rather than overshadow, the journey of inner growth and self-acceptance.

04
Personal and Organizational Development

> Success is doing ordinary things extraordinarily well.
>
> — Jim Rohn

HOLISTECH

For my entire career, I've explored the intricacies of the human mind and its quest for happiness and well-being. In the spirit of integrating the rich traditions of the past with the promises of the future, I identified three key pillars for personal enrichment: optimal wellness, enhanced cognitive performance, and graceful aging.

Over time, I realized that achieving personal growth wasn't merely about adopting specific techniques but about harnessing an empowered state of mind that enables conscious decision-making. Whether assisting individuals grappling with health challenges or guiding those at the zenith of success, the real reward was witnessing their metamorphosis from despair to empowerment through increased mindfulness of these pillars of enrichment.

Considering the broader picture, I realized that it was crucial to examine not just each individual, but also how those individuals function as part of larger systems, such as communities or organizations. As social creatures who spend so much of our time working and playing with others, we influence and are influenced by the cultures of the systems we inhabit. I couldn't ignore this interplay, so I pivoted focus to begin a journey into consulting for businesses and organizations.

To clarify my understanding of personal and collective dynamics, I embarked on a program at Harvard Business School, aspiring to fulfill my father's unachieved dream. This academic sojourn confirmed to me the symbiotic relationship between personal development and organizational leadership,

They are inseparable, two strands to the same helix

I learned that today it is indeed formally acknowledged that the mental and physical wellness of individuals is pivotal for nurturing vibrant teams. If the individual falters, an organization's performance inevitably wanes. Strikingly, despite rigorous financial analyses, quantifying human wellness and its impact on organizational performance remains challenging. Organizations often neglect these individual elements entirely, or else struggle to find effective strategies in nurturing them.

While concepts of 'company culture' and collective wellness aren't novel, many employees still hesitate to voice their struggles, fearing judgment or job loss. The responsibility then falls on leaders to prioritize this domain.

Further emphasizing this need was the COVID-19 pandemic, which brought a dramatic shift in work paradigms and personal perspectives.

Technology emerged as an essential ally. Digital tools made remote work viable, while telehealth platforms ensured access to well-being support. Digital learning platforms enabled continuous personal growth.

The changes forced by the pandemic, while daunting, also offered a silver lining. Organizations can now analyze the usage data of these tools and fine-tune their strategies moving forward, fostering both individual and collective improvement.

The experience prompted us all to ponder the true essence of work and life, reshaping our perspectives on success and well-being. It instilled a deeper sense of empathy and social awareness. Leaders began to realize that championing health could yield tangible benefits, from reducing burnout to attracting top-tier talent and nurturing a culture of innovation. As I've witnessed firsthand, the intersection of modern technology with a people-first approach paves the way for a future where individuals don't just work for a living, but find genuine fulfillment through their work.

HOLISTECH

The Surgeon General's Framework for Workplace Mental Health and Well-Being

During my studies, I was introduced to a workplace wellness model that bore striking similarities to Dr. Seligman's renowned PERMA model of happiness and well-being. Much like the PERMA Model, the Surgeon General's Framework emphasizes a holistic approach to workplace well-being, establishing it as an amalgamation of various factors that contribute to individual and collective wellness.

What is intriguing is how this model underscores the emphasis on specifically worker voice and equity. Each component of the model is rooted in two basic human needs, which remain consistent across diverse industries and roles:

Protection from Harm:
(Addressing the needs of Safety and Security)

This is not merely about safeguarding physical well-being, but also about allowing adequate periods of rest, openly promoting mental health, and practicing the norms of Diversity, Equity, Inclusion, and Accessibility (DEIA).

Work-Life Harmony:
(Addressing the needs of Autonomy and Flexibility)

This advocates for granting individuals greater autonomy in their work, urging flexible and predictable schedules, increased access to paid leave, and respect for the boundaries that demarcate work from personal time.

Mattering at Work:
(Addressing the needs of Dignity and Meaning)

At the heart of this component is the recognition of individual value, and its profound connection to organizational achievements. This usually involves encouraging the following a living wage; involving workers in workplace decisions; nurturing a culture that values gratitude and recognition; and tethering individual contributions to the broader organizational mission

Connection & Community:
(Addressing the needs of Social Support and Belonging)

A thriving workplace is built on the foundations of inclusion and belonging. This element calls for the creation of cultures that welcome diversity, foster trusted relationships, and celebrate collaboration and teamwork.

Opportunity for Growth:
(Addressing the needs of Learning and Accomplishment)

Progress and growth are essential for maintaining a sense of purpose. This component encourages workplaces to provide quality training, education, and mentoring, create equitable pathways for career advancement, and establish a framework for feedback that is both relevant and reciprocal.

Reimagining the workplace according to these essentials offers an integrated view of personal well-being and organizational success. The parallels between Dr. Seligman's PERMA Model and the Surgeon General's Framework cement the belief that happiness and well-being drive both personal development and organizational growth. As professionals and organizations reevaluate their priorities on a global scale, we see an evolving definition of success. These models can serve as guiding lights, illuminating the path to holistic well-being.

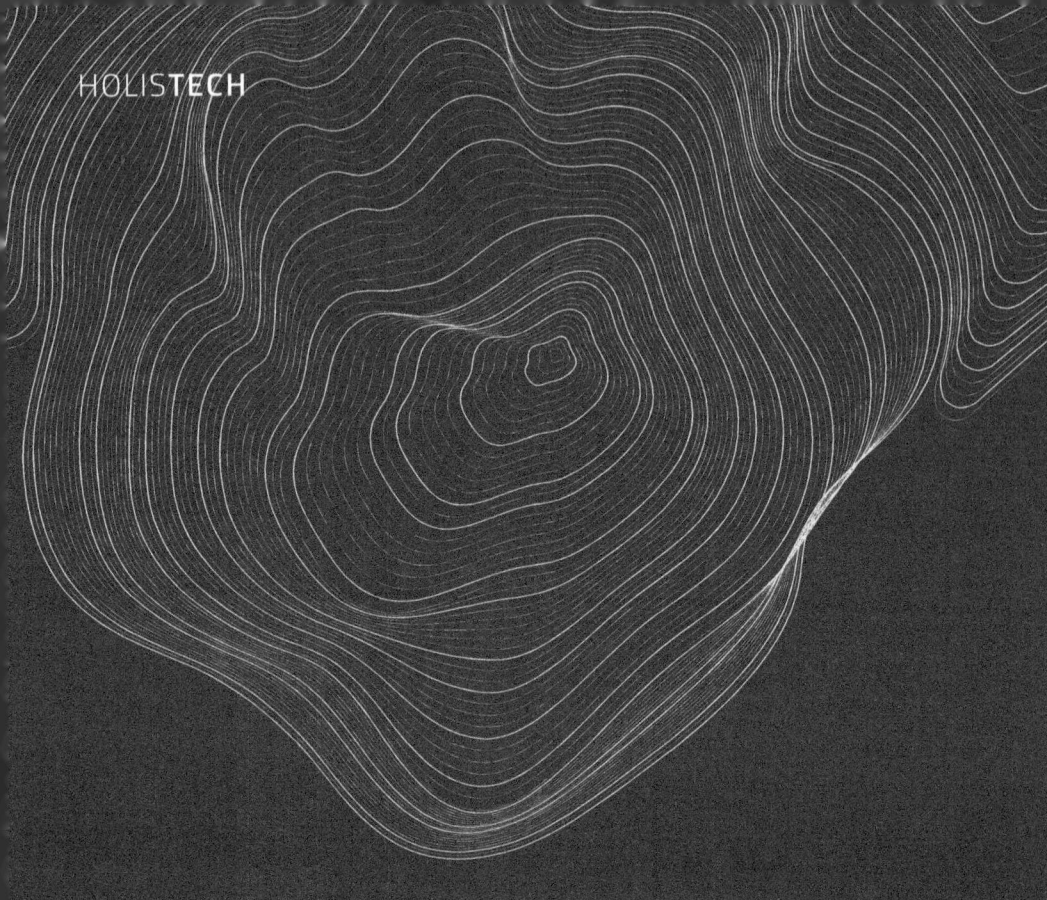

05
Authentic Human Connection and Development

> When a flower doesn't bloom, you fix the environment in which it grows, not the flower.

Alexander Den Heijer

HOLIS**TECH**

We've always been dreamers. From ancient legends to modern aspirations, our stories shimmer with desire for longevity, beauty, prosperity, power, and peace. Yet, even as we chase these dreams, the present moment—our lived experience—slips through our fingers. Why does this happen, especially when we stand on the shoulders of visionaries armed with cutting-edge technology?

Now more than ever, the call for personal development and systematic evolution is deafening. In a time starved for genuine human bonds, there's a palpable yearning to fill the void—to feel that we are good enough, we are part of something meaningful, we are safe and supported. These desires have been haunting us for millennia, yet still, invisible barriers hold us back from these personal and professional aspirations.

The Path to a Flourishing Life

From my practice I've found that any individual's journey to flourishing tends to require that certain elements converge—and that these elements often emerge in a particular order. If all goes well, this pattern of growth can replicate itself indefinitely across multiple domains of life, engendering a sense of personal agency and fulfillment. Unfortunately, today's world presents many obstacles that keep this cycle from unfolding in its natural way. In this section we'll explore four of the major barriers that hold us back, but first I'll briefly explain what happens in the best-case scenario:

The journey of personal growth begins with an awareness of the dream. Somehow, the spark is ignited: the primal knowledge of the value of life awakens or becomes revitalized. This may occur through some emergent event, or a gradual coming to terms. Regardless of its source, with this dream comes a desire to explore life's potential, to live it to its fullest and to flourish.

After ignition, the individual begins to establish authentic connections with others. This occurs through absorption into an existing community, or the deliberate curation of a social support network. These connections serve to inspire, open doors, and provide input whenever the path becomes foggy. It is ideal for this group to be diverse in thought and background, so the individual is guided toward their own highest potential instead of a path dictated by group biases and preconceptions.

Having a support system in place sets the stage for personal development in one or more domains that are currently relevant to the individual. This can take the form of formal, directed learning or informal exploration, practice, and mentorship. In any case, it is an accumulation of skill and awareness, expanding the potential for the person to act and contribute to the world.

Here again, diversity is critical. Throughout this book, I have described various elements of physical and mental health. To create a solid foundation for further personal and professional growth, it is essential to develop a certain level of competency in all of these essential domains of life skills. Out of necessity or ambition, many of my clients maximize their development admirably in some particular discipline, but this often comes at the expense of balanced personal growth. When someone takes time to nurture their holistic wellness while also growing in their chosen professional domain, they set themselves up for more resilient success.

It takes sacrifice, of course, and circumstances limit some of us far more than others. But even for those of us who feel the universe is against us, balance and consistency will always be better than the alternatives.

Finally, the individual applies what they've learned, and actively performs in their domains of choice. They begin to experience a state of peak performance. Because we always retain the capacity to learn and grow, this is a peak that can continuously rise higher. The more elements of well-being we have in place, the greater the performance.

The highest peaks of performance are attained by those who are fed by a deep reservoir of health and connection.

The Obstacles to Authentic Human Connection and Development

Despite its universal appeal through times and cultures, the story told above is not the norm. Many go through life without believing they can achieve anything beyond their current or 'designated' state. Others begin the journey enthusiastically, but face setbacks, abandoning the pursuit before it can bear fruit. Those who embrace the journey and successfully navigate their way to peak performance are few and far between.

Through my research and experience in my practice, I identified four formidable challenges, systemic and individual, that create a gap in the path to flourishing. Each of these obstacles can act as a roadblock that keeps an individual or organization from achieving their potential. Our ability to individually and collectively overcome these obstacles can unmistakably shape our personal and professional development, defining the extent of human flourishing we are able to achieve.

Obstacle 1: The Ideological and Generation Gap

Think of it as a silent divide. The Merriam-Webster dictionary paints it as the differences in views, values, and more, dividing young and the old. This divide is especially glaring within our contemporary social media landscapes, crafting quiet chasms of platform and content that pull generations away from mutual support and collaborative thinking.

From generation to generation, the passing down of wisdom has promoted stability and growth. Inasmuch as it stretches beyond the genetic intuition of animals, it is a uniquely human trait. We write books, tell stories, build religions up and tear them down. This is how we network with each other, and experiment to find the stable path. Today we are watching these eternal mechanisms change shape before our eyes. New landscapes are constantly emerging which require new skillsets and create new power dynamics. Those familiar with the existing terrain find a rift between them and those born in the new land. Often these rifts form along generational lines, and confuse the flow of knowledge. It is tempting for one generation to dismiss the experience of another as irrelevant or naïve, but doing so would be to miss out any potential for integration and connection.

We've also heard about people being trapped within their "ideological bubbles," with social media exacerbating this by feeding people more content that aligns with content they've previously chosen to view. As face-to-face interaction plummets and more media is consumed through algorithmically-generated channels, these bubbles can become a person's entire world of information and connections. In this state it becomes easier to label an "us" and a "them" and a "good" and a "bad" in every domain of life, obscuring the nuances of a situation and diminishing the growth mindset we need to learn together.

People do vary in their tendency to focus on discrete classifications and labels. For instance, research tells us that members of the Silent Generation and Baby Boomers often resonate more with their generational labels than their younger counterparts. In the social media realm, these labels and ideologies (whether externally or self-imposed) are brought inexorably to the forefront of attention. This creates unavoidable division.

Oftentimes it seems as though we've unconsciously sculpted digital spaces that limit connectivity and growth.

Bridging the generational and ideological expanse isn't a walk in the park. For true engagement, and to birth meaningful personal and organizational growth, we need spaces marked by open-mindedness and compassion. It's crucial for everyone to feel comfortable enough to share their stories, insights, and unique worldviews.

Obstacle 2: Lack of Happiness, Meaning and Purpose

The second challenge I encountered was the pervasive lack of happiness, meaning, or purpose that keeps people from feeling motivated to excel. The American Freshman Survey National Norms suggests that the importance ascribed to "Developing a Meaningful Philosophy of Life" has seen a decrease of 34 percent, dropping from 86% in 1967 to 52% in 2005 and by the fall of 2019, it further slipped to 50%.

Notably, this 2019 figure was captured before the onset of the global COVID-19 pandemic. Given the profound societal and personal changes brought about by the pandemic, one might reasonably assume that the subsequent scores could dip even lower as students' priorities and perspectives continue to evolve in response to global challenges.

While technological advancements are reshaping human connections, there are unanticipated consequences to consider. Among them is the escalation of Social Comparison, which has been linked to increased unhappiness, depression, and feelings of disconnection. This phenomenon affects us all, often subtly shaping our perception of our world on a daily basis.

Consider the current digital landscape. Unrestricted and unending access does not always translate into authentic connections or clearly defined goals. We are often exposed to influencers showcasing a luxury lifestyle, infinite leisure time, and constant competitive display. There are thousands of analysts and programmers working around the clock to figure out the human mind, to shove each and every one of us (through individualized, meticulously-tailored media) toward material consumption in the pursuit of happiness. The conscious and subconscious perceptions formed through these interactions significantly influence our self-image, the ways we pursue happiness, and how we define our life purpose. The impact of social comparisons is even more profound on younger generations, which show a decreased interest in defining a meaningful life purpose of any sort.

Beyond the digital, there are many other modern contributing factors to a lack of happiness, meaning, and purpose. These might include materialism, work-life imbalance, environmental concerns, political and social uncertainty, loss of community and traditions, and information overload. These examples paint a picture of a challenging interplay of societal and technological factors that each of us must navigate through our pursuit of a flourishing life.

Obstacle 3: Absence of a Supporting Environment

The third significant challenge I identified through the research and my direct observation with clients is the glaring absence of an environment conducive to support and growth.

I've long felt that a fundamental component of both personal and workplace development is psychological safety, defined as the shared belief within a group or organization that it is safe to take interpersonal risks without fear of negative consequences or reprisals. In a psychologically safe environment, individuals feel comfortable expressing their thoughts, ideas, concerns, and feedback openly, without the fear of ridicule or retaliation.

My studies in the Harvard Organizational Development program reinforced the criticality of this element in organizations. Their research confirms that businesses emphasizing psychological safety see higher engagement and innovation from their teams, resulting in lower turnover. Establishing such an environment goes beyond merely averting conflicts. It actively shields those who might feel marginalized, stimulates innovation, amplifies underrepresented voices, and brings clarity to everyone's responsibilities and roles.

Codified, the key components of psychological safety include:

1. **Trust:** Team members trust that their colleagues and leaders will treat them with respect and empathy, even when they express differing opinions or make mistakes.
2. **Open Communication:** People feel encouraged to voice their thoughts, share feedback, and ask questions without hesitation.
3. **Non-judgmental Atmosphere:** The culture does not stigmatize mistakes or differences in perspective. Instead, it values learning and growth.
4. **Inclusivity:** Everyone, regardless of their background or identity, feels equally respected and included, contributing to a sense of belonging.
5. **Supportive Leadership:** Leaders play a crucial role in fostering psychological safety by modeling inclusive behavior, actively listening, and addressing concerns constructively.

Within such nurturing spaces, individuals are emboldened to voice their thoughts, venture beyond their comfort zones, and channel their creativity freely. This cultivates a fertile ground where growth is not merely encouraged but inevitable. This harmonious balance can be difficult to maintain however, given the myriad challenges posed by cultural differences, biases around disabilities, and the potential for misinterpretation.

I do not meet many people who have a psychologically safe environment both at home and work. Especially in the workplace, this element is unfortunately often outside the direct control of the individual, leaving them limited options beyond leaving to seek a safer environment elsewhere. Fortunately for leaders, there are many efficient ways to build psychological safety within a group that can keep their team content and developing toward peak performance.

Obstacle 4: Developmental Misconceptions

The fourth challenge is one I identified over time through my diverse studies of personal and organizational development. It became apparent that certain fundamental misconceptions within our current understanding of these subjects have been posing significant impediments to holistic growth in both individuals and organizations.

These misconceptions tend to distort the value and effectiveness of a well-rounded consultation, and can misdirect an otherwise effective attempt at development. They revolve predominantly around four pivotal aspects: communication; diversity and inclusion; knowledge; and technology.

Misconception about Communication:

It's a commonly held belief that communication is merely the exchange of information. The reality is it's far more layered. I eventually realized in my consultations that I needed to grasp not only people's informational needs but also their underlying desires and intentions. This was reflected in my clients' family dynamics as well. When I encouraged my clients to communicate with their family members, doctors, or organizations, they often assumed that merely delivering their message sufficed. What they failed to grasp was that effective communication is not as straightforward as saying, "I just need some time to myself." This oversight often led to confusion or a lack of compassion in their delivery, resulting in lengthy or unproductive discussions.

Within organizational contexts, a frequent example is a misunderstanding of how to effectively communicate personal boundaries. Consider a scenario where an employee receives an urgent email from a supervisor during their personal time. Without a clear understanding of how to communicate their boundaries, the employee might feel pressured to respond immediately, even though they have valid reasons for not doing so. This lack of communication can lead to stress and frustration for the employee, and potentially affect their overall well-being and work-life balance.

Think of communication not as a mere relay of facts, but as the collaborative process of building a bridge. Just as two shores are connected by a bridge, so are two individuals when they communicate effectively. It's about mutual construction on a shared foundation, not just one side laying bricks in thin air.' In my consultations, I often underscore this point. Consultation is not about talking; it's about forging connections through dialogue; emphasizing active listening; mutual understanding of the problem and the desired outcome; and, above all, empathy.

During an insightful lecture on leadership at Harvard by Dr. Joshua Margolis and Dr. Tony Mayo, I was introduced to the details of "Communicating Direction." The core takeaway? Communication is not solely reliant on content, but also on its delivery. It's not just what you communicate but how you bring it across. If you want to rally others behind a vision, they must not only understand it but be enthused to make it their own. It is vital that everyone feels aligned and properly recognized in the space of shared vision or discussion.

To simplify, consider Harvard's Five Lenses of Communication:
- **Audience:** It's not about a one-size-fits-all message. Dive deep to understand who you're speaking to. What do they feel? How might they react?
- **Content:** Your message's heart. What's the core idea you want them to take away?
- **Purpose:** Why are you communicating? Is it to inform, to inspire, or perhaps to initiate a dialogue?
- **Process:** The channels and rhythm of your communication. How often and through which medium will you connect?
- **Tone or Style:** Beyond words, it's about how you come across—the emotions you stir, the body language, the unsaid cues."

Harvard also suggests that for an impactful communication style, it is important to remember this six Cs:

- "**Compassion:** Connect emotionally, understand deeply.
- **Clarity:** Speak so even a novice can grasp the message.
- **Conciseness:** Be precise, avoid overwhelming.
- **Connection:** Create a bond that transcends the spoken word.
- **Conviction:** Speak with passion and unwavering belief.
- **Courage:** Have the fortitude to voice even the unpopular opinions."

In essence, my education and subsequent practice have taught me that communication transcends mere information exchange. It's about igniting passion, stimulating thought, and inspiring change or mutual understanding. Many roadblocks on the path to flourishing can only be sufficiently resolved through skillful communication.

Misconception about Knowledge:

The G.I. Joe Fallacy, named after the iconic action figure and animated series G.I. Joe, perpetuated the mistaken idea that "knowing" is enough to change your behavior. In the world of G.I. Joe, this concept was encapsulated by the catchphrase "Knowing is half the battle," which implied that once you had the knowledge, you were well on your way to victory. However, my journey in the fall of 2019, when I enrolled in Yale University's esteemed course, "The Science of Well-Being," under the guidance of Dr. Laurie Santos, shed light on the fallacy's profound implications, as both Santos and Tamar Gendler brilliantly articulated it.

The essence of the G.I. Joe Fallacy lies in the understanding that the mere acquisition of knowledge isn't transformational by itself. It's the bridge between understanding and action that catalyzes real change. In simpler terms, knowing represents only half of the equation. To truly enrich our lives, we must actively apply the knowledge we've gained.

This paradigm shift in understanding proved invaluable in my consulting sessions, where my clients and I emphasized the importance of transitioning from theoretical insights to tangible actions. Together, we shared a clear objective: to cultivate not only a comprehensive understanding but also the essential tools to manifest personal and professional aspirations.

Upon reflection, the insights derived from the G.I. Joe Fallacy have played a foundational role in refining both my consultancy approach and my course development. They serve as a testament to my commitment: to ensure that knowledge doesn't merely illuminate the mind but also fuels transformative action in our everyday existence. I believe this same commitment serves as invaluable grounding for any journey toward the dream of a flourishing life.

Misconception about Diversity and Inclusion:

In 2019, determined to further diversify my knowledge on personal development and organizational leadership, I also enrolled in the "High Performance Collaboration: Leadership, Teamwork, and Negotiation" course at Northwestern University, led by the distinguished Dr. Leigh Thompson. This experience was more than just an academic pursuit; it was a quest to gain a profound understanding of Diversity & Inclusion (D&I) that extended beyond its surface interpretations. Through this enlightening course, I came to realize that there are several common misconceptions about D&I that, if not rectified, can keep individuals and organizations from being able to express their potential.

6. **Limited to Demographics:** One prevalent misconception is that diversity and inclusion primarily pertain to demographic attributes such as race, gender, or age. However, I learned that true D&I goes beyond these visible traits and encompasses a rich tapestry of differences in thought, experience, and cognitive approaches. It's about celebrating the unique perspectives each individual brings to the table.
7. **Surface-Level Understanding:** Many people mistakenly believe that acknowledging diversity is sufficient for fostering inclusion. This oversimplified view fails to recognize that genuine inclusion requires active efforts to create an environment where diverse voices are heard, valued, and integrated into decision-making processes.

8. **Ignoring Cognitive Diversity:** Another misconception is overlooking the significance of cognitive diversity within D&I efforts. Diversity in thought processes, problem-solving approaches, and decision-making styles is just as crucial as demographic diversity. Embracing cognitive diversity can lead to more innovative solutions and better overall team performance.
9. **Homogeneity in Networks:** Some assume that effective networks should consist of like-minded individuals who share the same perspectives and experiences. In reality, open-looped networks that encompass a diverse range of individuals with distinct knowledge and expertise can be more powerful. These networks encourage varied thinking styles and profound experiences, fostering a broader perspective.
10. **Assimilation Over Integration:** A common misunderstanding is that D&I initiatives aim to assimilate individuals into a standardized culture. However, the true essence of D&I is about integrating diverse thought processes and experiences into the existing culture. It's not about conformity but about creating an environment that encourages individuality and innovation.
11. **Static State of Inclusion:** Many organizations wrongly view inclusion as a static achievement rather than an ongoing process. In reality, fostering inclusion requires continuous efforts and a commitment to adapt to changing demographics, perspectives, and societal dynamics.

Drawing upon these insights I realized that true human connection and development is about embracing diversity in all its forms, actively fostering inclusion, and valuing the richness of differing perspectives and experiences. It is my hope that by challenging these misconceptions, organizations can create environments that harness the full potential of their diverse teams to drive holistic innovation, while individuals can be better prepared to advocate for the inclusion of their own unique perspective into this unfolding story of growth.

Misconceptions about Technology:

My dedication to understanding the intricacies of life and its challenges led me to a surprising juncture in a serene yoga studio. In this space of meditation and movement, one attendee, Benjamin, stood out. His precise postures and

HOLISTECH

focused demeanor hinted at his profession even before we spoke: a mechanical engineer. But Benjamin (my soon-to-be life partner) wasn't there just for physical alignment; he was exploring the very mechanics of his existence.

As the class ended and the gentle hum of the studio settled, Benjamin approached with an invitation: tea and a conversation about our respective perceptions of reality. What unfolded was a spirited dialogue intertwining his technological insights with my background in humanities and personal development. That conversation symbolized more than just an exchange of ideas; it represented the convergence of two minds, two worlds, and two disciplines. Having traveled vast distances to find myself in that very moment, I was reminded of the serendipitous beauty of life's journey.

During our dynamic conversations, Benjamin and I found ourselves at the intersection of ancient wisdom and modern innovation. The fluidity of our dialogues highlighted the juxtaposition of our backgrounds: mine, grounded in the humanities and personal development, and his, in the precision and analytical nature of engineering. As we delved deeper into our discussions, a recurrent theme began to emerge: the transformative power of technology and its role in elevating and evolving—rather than usurping—ancient principles and ideas.

Take, for instance, the profound philosophies underpinning yoga. At its core, yoga is about connection — to oneself, to others, and to the universe. But what if we could leverage technology to deepen this connection, to make it more tangible and accessible in our modern age? Benjamin's insights into the latest technological advancements began to shed light on potential integrations. We speculated about the use of wearable technology to track and improve postural alignment; or virtual reality to enhance meditative experiences, transporting practitioners to idyllic dreamscapes for deeper introspection.

As our conversations expanded, we started recognizing that this amalgamation of technology with traditional concepts wasn't just exclusive to our personal interests. In professional realms, technology was breaking barriers and enhancing understanding in unprecedented ways. The ability to simulate complex scenarios, gather vast amounts of data for analysis, or even use augmented reality for skill development were transforming industries.

But perhaps the most profound realization was in the realm of education and knowledge dissemination. The principles that have remained largely unchanged for centuries were now accessible in more interactive and engaging formats, thanks to technology. Complex concepts were being broken down and visualized using advanced graphics, making them easier to grasp. Practical knowledge, which traditionally required hands-on experience, could now be simulated through virtual environments, allowing learners to practice and perfect their skills without real-world consequences.

It became evident that technology wasn't just a tool for efficiency; it was a bridge. A bridge that connected traditional wisdom with modern needs, a bridge that made abstract concepts tangible, and a bridge that democratized access to knowledge and practical skills. Through our dialogues, Benjamin and I realized that to truly honor and expand upon the wisdom of the past, we needed to embrace the tools of the present and future.

Years later, the vibrant memories of our first tea-fueled conversation still echo in our lives. Despite the whirlwind of changes, advancements, and new responsibilities, one tradition remains untouched: our "tea time." We consider it a sacred ritual. Whether it's a lazy Sunday afternoon or a quick evening breather after a hectic day, we brew our favorite teas and delve into conversation.

Sometimes we reminisce about our early debates and speculations, marveling at how some of them have now manifested in reality. Sometimes we discuss the latest technological advancements, and ponder their implications on society, education, and personal development. And often, amidst the steam and delicate aromas, we simply share our day, our idle thoughts, and our dreams.

This ritual is our anchor. It constantly reminds us of the importance of connection, reflection, and continuous learning. In a world that's rapidly evolving, our tea time serves as a beautiful testament to the value of tradition. It's a blend of the old and the new, much like our initial discussions; and it's a tradition we hold close, ensuring we never lose sight of where we started and where we aspire to go.

Surpassing the Obstacles

Unlike G.I. Joe, I see knowing as the start of the battle, or perhaps a method of avoiding all but the necessary battles. I share these obstacles to human connection and development not to intimidate, but to shed more light on the road ahead as it exists in today's ever-changing world. With awareness of the pitfalls, it is easier

HOLISTECH

to take each new challenge in stride and seize each frustration as an opportunity for growth. As we've seen, it is easy to become disenchanted with the mere idea of living a purposeful life, but if we can revel in the journey as the destination, we can more joyfully experience each step in its own full potential.

Reflecting Upon the Journey

From the time I was a young girl, my imagination has been the canvas upon which vibrant images danced and grand scenarios unfurled. Frequently, I would lose myself in a mental expedition, fantasizing about an evening spent with the most profound thinkers and pure-hearted individuals to have ever graced humanity. In this intriguing reverie, I would ask myself: What topics would draw them in, spark their curiosity? How did they manage to live a flourishing life, or did they at all? How would they tackle the eternal conundrums that have kept the brightest scientists, philosophers, artists, and mystics at their wit's end?

In the stage of my mind's theater, these extraordinary figures—a mix of the ancients and the contemporaries—convened at a time-travelers' round table. Their goal was never mere intellectual display, but active discussion on the questions that have long puzzled mankind. They strove to reach a shared understanding, perhaps even a consensus.

As I embarked on my consulting journey, a recurring theme surfaced: diverse minds craved a lingua franca—a bridge—to genuinely connect, especially when navigating complex realms like personal growth, professional evolution, and the essence of human connection.

It was during this period that I encountered the compelling science of human connection and development. This paradigm had the potency to crystallize discussions into actionable blueprints, anchored in scientifically vetted knowledge.

At its heart, this ideology treats both human life and organizations as dynamic systems, primed for evolution and refinement through evidence-driven strategies. Central to this scientific ideology is the recognition that human interactions and group dynamics adhere to identifiable patterns. These patterns, when understood and harnessed, can uplift everyone involved.

As we conclude our exploration of group processes and personal growth, it's vital to recognize that every experience, every bit of knowledge, is a stepping stone to more profound realizations. Just as the end of a course serves as a launching pad into new horizons, so too has my development of this book.

Every narrative, insight, and epiphany shared within the pages of Holistech has been a step that guided me to a critical crossroads in my own journey.

HOLISTECH

Through these explorations—both personal and organizational—I've witnessed the extraordinary alignment of wellbeing principles with the latest advances in technology. This fascinating intersection ignited a fervor within me, inspiring me to challenge the perceived limits of our work culture and personal lives. I see a landscape brimming with untapped potential—from optimizing our physical prowess and mental fortitude to embracing the promise of a gracefully enriched future. This melding has flung open the doors to innovation, urging me to explore, pioneer, and craft new paths for both individuals and organizations to flourish in a world that's in constant flux.

The chapters may end, but our journey is ceaseless. Every insight, every challenge surmounted, and every horizon yet to be explored adds to the richness of our shared mission. We're not just mapping out paths; we're creating legacies.

We are shaping a world with fewer and fewer limits to transformation.

I want to express my sincere gratitude for your unwavering support, dedication, and belief in this extraordinary mission. As we move forward, let's remember that our journey is a lifelong commitment to continual growth and evolution. In transforming ourselves, we become beacons of hope and inspiration for others.

Together, we will face challenges with grace and resilience, reminding ourselves that our journey has the potential to reshape the world in unimaginable ways. Our journey is far from over; it is an ongoing adventure that calls for embracing uncertainty, adapting to change, and continually pushing our boundaries.

It is through these moments of growth and self-discovery that we truly tap into our potential. Let us press on, exploring uncharted territories, pushing boundaries, and creating new possibilities.

The adventure, undoubtedly, continues.

References

This section lists material referenced in creation of both the *Holistech* book and the Metamind Program described herein.

•

Alberts, H. J.E.M., Thewissen, R, & Raes, L. (2012). Dealing with problematic eating behavior. The effects of a mindfulness-based intervention on eating behavior, food cravings, dichotomous thinking and body image concern, Appetite, 58, 847–851.

Alberts, H., Schneider, F., & Martijn., C. (2012). Dealing efficiently with emotions: Acceptance-based Coping with Negative Emotions Requires Fewer resources than Suppression. Cognition and Emotion, 26, 863-70.

Arch, J. J., & Craske, M. G. (2006). Mechanisms of mindfulness: Emotion regulation following a focused breathing induction. Behaviour Research and Therapy, 44, 1849-1858.

Baer, R. A. (2003). Mindfulness training as clinical intervention: A conceptual and empirical review. Clinical Psychology: Science and Practice, 10, 125–143.

Baer, R. A., Smith, G. T., Hopkins, J., Krietemeyer, J., & Toney, L. (2006). Using self-report assessment methods to explore facets of mindfulness. Assessment, 13, 27–45.

Baker, L. R., & McNulty, J. K. (2011, January 31). Self-Compassion and Relationship Maintenance: The Moderating Roles of Conscientiousness and Gender. Journal of Personality and Social Psychology. Advance online publication.

Baumeister, R. F., & Leary, M. R. (1995). The need to belong: Desire for interpersonal attachments as a fundamental human motivation. Psychological Bulletin, 117, 497–529.

Baumeister, R. F., Bratslavsky, E., Muraven, M., & Tice, D. M. (1998). Ego depletion: Is the active self a limited resource? Journal of Personality and Social Psychology, 74, 1252- 1265.

Baumeister, R. F., Heatherton, T. F., & Tice, D. M. (1994). Losing control: How and why people fail at self-regulation. San Diego, CA: Academic Press.

Baumeister, R., & Leary, M. R. (1995). The need to belong: Desire for interpersonal attachments as a fundamental human motivation. Psychological Bulletin, 117, 497–529.

Boekaerts,M. (1999). Self-regulated learning. Wherewe are today. International Journal of Educational Research, 31, 445–457.

Brach, T. (2016, August). How to start a mindfulness meditation group. Retrieved from www.tarabrach.com

Brickman, P. and D.T. Campbell: 1971, Hedonic relativism and planning the good society, in M.H. Appley (ed.), Adaptation-level Theory (Academic Press, New York), pp. 287-302.

Brickman, P., Coates, D., & Jano-Bulman, R. (1978) Lottery winners and accident victims: Is happiness relative? Journal of Personality and Social Psychology, 36, 917-927.

Brown, K. W., & Ryan, R. M. (2003). The benefits of being present: Mindfulness and its role in psychological well-being. Journal of Personality and Social Psychology, 84, 822-848.

Brown, K. W., Ryan, R. M., & Creswell, J. D. (2007). Mindfulness: Theoretical foundations and evidence for its salutary effects. Psychological Inquiry, 18, 272– 281.

Brown, S. L., Nesse, R. M., Vinokur, A. D., & Smith, D. M. (2003). Providing social support may be more beneficial than receiving it: Results from a prospective study of mortality. Psychological Science,14, 320– 327.

Cahn, B. R., & Polich, J. (2009). Meditation (Vipassana) and the P3a event-related brain potential. International Journal of Psychophysiology, 72, 51–60.

Cardaciotto, L., Herbert, J. D., Forman, E. M., Moitra, E., & Farrow, V. (2008). The assessment of present-moment awareness and acceptance: The Philadelphia Mindfulness Scale. Assessment, 15, 204–223.

Carson, J. W., Keefe, F. J., Lynch, T. R., Carson, K. M., Goli, V., Fras, A. M., et al. (2005). Loving-kindness meditation for chronic low back pain: results from a pilot trial. Journal of Holistic Nursing, 23, 287–304.

Carver, C. S. (2004). Self-regulation of action and affect. In R. F. Baumeister & K. D. Vohs (Eds.), Handbook of self-regulation: Research, theory, and applications (pp. 13-39). New York: Guilford.

Chambers, R., Lo, B. C. Y., & Allen, N. B. (2008). The impact of intensive mindfulness training on attentional control, cognitive style, and affect. Cognitive Therapy and Research, 32, 303–322.

Cialdini, R. B., Borden, R. J., Thorne, A., Walker, M. R., Freeman, S., & Sloan, L. R. (1976). Basking in reflected glory: Three (football) field studies. Journal of Personality and Social Psychology, 34, 366–375.

Cialdini, R. B., Brown, S. L., Lewis, B. P., Luce, C., & Neuberg, S. L. (1997). Reinterpreting the empathy-altruism relationship: When one into one equals oneness. Journal of Personality and Social Psychology, 73, 481–494.

Condon, P., & DeSteno, D., (2011). Compassion for one reduces punishment for another. Journal of Experimental Social Psychology, 47, 698–701.

Crocker, J., & Park, L. E. (2004). The costly pursuit of self-esteem. Psychological Bulletin, 130, 392–414.

Crocker, J., Karpinski, A., Quinn, D. M., & Chase, S. K. (2003). When grades determine self-worth: Consequences of contingent self-worth for male and female engineering and psychology majors. Journal of Personality and Social Psychology, 85, 507-516.

Cullen, M., Pons, G. B., & Mindful Staff. (2016, January 25). Mindfulness of anger. Retrieved from www.mindful.org/mindfulness-of-anger/

De Vries, A. C., Glasper, E. R., & Detillion, C. E. (2003). Social modulation of stress responses. Physiology and Behavior, 79, 399–407.

Deci, E. L., & Ryan, R. M. (1995). Human autonomy: The basis for true self-esteem. In M. Kernis (Ed.), Efficacy, agency, and self-esteem (pp. 31-49). New York: Plenum.

Deci, E. L., & Ryan, R. M. (2000). The 'what' and 'why' of goal pursuits: Human needs and the self-determination of behavior. Psychological Inquiry, 11, 319–338.

Deikman, A.J. (1982). The observing self. Boston: Beacon Press.

Desimone, R., & Duncan, J. (1995). Neural mechanisms of selective visual attention. Annual Reviews of Neuroscience, 18, 193–222.

Developmental Psychology, 34, 403–419.

Drake, L., Duncan, E., Sutherland, F., Abernethy, C., & Henry, C. (2008). Time Perspective and Correlates of Well-Being. Time and Society, 17, 47–61.

Dubert, C. J., Schumacher, A. M., Locker, L., Gutierrez, A. P., & Barnes, V. A. (2016). Mindfulness and emotion regulation among nursing students: Investigating the mediation effect of working memory capacity. Mindfulness 7, 1061-1070.

Duckworth, A. L., & Seligman, M. E. (2005). Self-discipline outdoes IQ in predicting academic performance of adolescents. Psychological Science, 16, 939–944.

Emmons, R.A., & McCullough, M.E. (2003). Counting blessings versus burdens: An experimental investigation of gratitude and subjective well-being in daily life. Journal of Personality and Social Psychology 84, 377-389.

Enriquez-Geppert, S., Huster, R. J., & Herrmann, C. S. (2013). Boosting brain functions: Improving executive functions with behavioral training, neurostimulation, and neurofeedback. International journal of psychophysiology, 88(1), 1-16.

Extinguish addiction with mindfulness. (2016). Retrieved from www.mindfulmuscle.com

Feldman, G., Hayes, A., Kumar, S., Greeson, J., & Laurenceau, J. (2007). Mindfulness and emotion regulation: The development and initial validation of the Cognitive and Affective Mindfulness Scale-Revised (CAMS-R). Journal of Psychopathology and Behavioral Assessment, 29, 177–190.

Fetterman, A. K., Robinson, M. D., Ode, S. et al. (2010). Neuroticism as a risk factor for behavioral dysregulation: A mindfulness mediation perspective. Journal of Social and Clinical Psychology, 29, 301-321.

Fleming, J. E., & Kocovski, N. L. (2007). Mindfulness and acceptance-based group therapy for social anxiety disorder: A treatment manual.

Flook, L., Goldberg, S. B., Pinger, L., & Davidson, R. J. (2015). Promoting prosocial behavior and self-regulatory skills in preschool children through a mindfulness-based kindness curriculum. Developmental Psychology, 51(1), 44.

Frederick, S. & Loewenstein, G. (1999) Hedonic adaptation, in D. Kahneman, E. Diener and N. Schwarz (eds), Well-being: The foundations of hedonic psychology (Russell Sage Foundation, New York), pp. 302-329.

Frewen, P. A., Evans, E. M., Maraj, N., Dozois, D. J. A., & Partridge, K. (2008). Letting go: Mindfulness and negative automatic thinking. Cognitive Therapy and Research, 32, 758-774.

Glaeser, E. L., Laibson, D. I., Scheinkman, J. A., & Soutter, C. L. (2000). Measuring trust. The Quarterly Journal of Economics, 115, 811–846.

Greenberg, J., Pyszczynski, T., Solomon, S., Simon, L., & Breus, M. (1994). Role of consciousness and accessibility of death-related thoughts in mortality salience effects. Journal of Personality and Social Psychology, 67, 627–637.

Greenberg, J., Solomon, S., & Pyszczynski, T. (1997). Terror management theory of self-esteem and social behavior: Empirical assessments and conceptual refinements. In M. P. Zanna (Ed.), Advances in experimental social psychology (Vol. 29, pp. 61–139). San Diego, CA: Academic Press.

Greeson J, Brantley J. (2009). Mindfulness and anxiety disorders: Developing a wise relationship with the inner experience of fear. In: Didonna F, editor. Clinical handbook of mindfulness. New York, NY: Springer; pp. 171–188. in press.

Grossman P., Niemann L., Schmidt S., Walach H. (2004), Mindfulness-based stress reduction and health benefits: A meta-analysis. Journal of Psychosomatic Research 57, 35-43.

Hagger, M. S., Wood, C., Stiff, C., & Chatzisarantis, N. L. D. (2010). Ego-depletion and the strength model of self-control: A meta-analysis. Psychological Bulletin, 136, 495-525.

Hawkley, L. C., Masi, C. M., Berry, J. D., & Cacioppo, J. T. (2006). Loneliness is a unique predictor of age-related differences in systolic blood pressure. Psychology and Aging, 21, 152–164.

Hofmann, G. (2013). Using mindfulness to treat anxiety disorders. Retrieved from www.psychcentral.com/blog/archives/2013/01/28/using-mindfulness-to-treat-anxiety-disorders/

Hofmann, S. G., Sawyer, A. T., Witt, A. A., & Oh, D. (2010). The effect of mindfulness-based therapy on anxiety and depression: A meta-analytic review. Journal of Consulting and Clinical Psychology, 78, 169-183.

Hutcherson, C. A., Seppala, E. M. & Gross, J. J. (2008). Loving-kindness meditation increases social connectedness. Emotion, 8, 720-724.

International Journal of Behavioral Consultation and Therapy 9(2), 1-3.

Iskender, M. (2009). The relationship between self-compassion, self-efficacy, and control beliefs about learning in Turkish university students. Social Behavior and Personality, 37, 711–720.

Jennings, J. L., & Apsche, J. A. (2014). The evolution of a fundamentally mindfulness-based treatment methodology: From DBT and ACT to MDT and beyond.

Jha, A. P., Krompinger, J., & Baime, M. J. (2007). Mindfulness training modifies subsystems of attention. Cognitive, Affective, and Behavioral Neuroscience, 7, 109–119.

Kelly, E. L., & Conley, J. J. (1987). Personality and compatibility: A prospective analysis of marital stability and marital satisfaction. Journal of Personality and Social Psychology, 52, 27–40.

Kober, S. E., Hinterleitner, V., Bauernfeind, G., Neuper, C., & Wood, G. (2018). Trainability of hemodynamic parameters: a near-infrared spectroscopy based neurofeedback study. Biological Psychology, 136, 168-180.

Kocovski, N. L., Fleming, J. E., Hawley, L. L., Huta, V., & Antony, M. M. (2013). Mindfulness and acceptance-based group therapy versus traditional cognitive-behavioral group therapy for social anxiety disorder: A randomized controlled trial. Behaviour Research and Therapy, 51, 889-898.

Kohl, S. H., Mehler, D. M., Lührs, M., Thibault, R. T., Konrad, K., & Sorger, B. (2020). The potential of functional near-infrared spectroscopy-based neurofeedback—a systematic review and recommendations for best practice. Frontiers in neuroscience, 14, 594.

Leary, M. R., Tate, E. B., Adams, C. E., Allen, A. B., & Hancock, J. (2007). Self-compassion and reactions to unpleasant self-relevant events: The implications of treating oneself kindly. Journal of Personality and Social Psychology, 92, 887– 904.

Leary, M., Adams, C., & Tate, E., 2006, Hypo-egoic self-regulation: Exercising self-control by diminishing the influence of the self. Journal of Personality, 74, 1803-1831.

Lee, R. M., & Robbins, S. B. (1998). The relationship between social connectedness and anxiety, self-esteem, and social identity. Journal of Counseling Psychology, 5, 338–345.

Linehan, M. M. (1993). Cognitive-Behavioral Treatment of Borderline Personality Disorder. New York: Guilford Press.

Locke, E.A., & Latham, G.P. (1990). A theory of goal setting and task performance. Englewood Cliffs, NJ: Prentice-Hall.

Locke, E.A.,& Latham, G.P. (2002). Building a practically useful theory of goal setting and task motivation: A 35-year odyssey. American Psychologist, 57, 705– 717.

Lutz, A., Slagter, H. A., Dunne, J. D., & Davidson, R. J. (2008). Attention regulation and monitoring in meditation. Trends in Cognitive Sciences, 12, 163–169.

McCullough, M. E., Emmons, R. A., & Tsang, J. (2002). The grateful disposition: A conceptual and empirical topography. Journal of Personality and Social Psychology, 82, 112–127.

Mindfulness meditation for addiction cravings. (2017). Retrieved from www.alcoholrehab.com Nauman, E. (2014, June 2). Three ways mindfulness reduces depression. Retrieved from www.greatergood.berkeley.edu

Moore, A., & Malinowski, P. (2009). Meditation, mindfulness and cognitive flexibility. Consciousness and Cognition, 18, 176–186.

Neff, K. D. (2003). Development and validation of a scale to measure self-compassion. Self and Identity, 2, 223–250.

Neff, K. D. (2004). Self-compassion and psychological well-being. Constructivism in the Human Sciences, 9, 27–37.

Neff, K. D., Hsieh, Y.-P., & Dejitterat, K. (2005). Self-compassion, achievement goals, and coping with academic failure. Self and Identity, 4, 263–287.

Neff, K. D.,Kirkpatrick, K. L., & Rude, S. S. (2007). Self-compassion and adaptive psychological functioning. Journal of Research in Personality, 41, 139–154.

Newsome, S., Waldo, M., & Gruszka, C. (2012). Mindfulness group work: Preventing stress and increasing self-compassion among helping professionals in training. The Journal for Specialists in Group Work, 1-15.

Niemiec, C. P., Brown, K. W., Kashdan, T. B., Cozzolino, P. J., Breen, W. E., Levesque, C. S., & Ryan, R. M. (2010). Being present in the face of existential threat: The role of trait mindfulness in reducing defensive responses to mortality salience. Journal of Personality and Social Psychology, 99, 344- 365.

Norman, D. A., & Shallice, T. (1986). Attention to action. In R. J. Davidson, G. E. Schwartz, & D. Shapiro (Eds.). Consciousness and self-regulation (Vol. 4, pp. 1–18). New York: Plenum.

Oaten, M., & Cheng, K. (2006). Improved self-control: The benefits of a regular program of academic study. Basic and Applied Social Psychology, 28, 1-16.

Overwalle, F. V., Mervielde, I., & De Schuyter, J. (1995). Structural modeling of the relationships between attributional dimensions, emotions, and performance of college freshmen. Cognition & Emotion, 9, 59–85.

Raes, F., Dewulf, D., Van Heeringen, C., Williams, J.M.G. (2009). Mindfulness and reduced cognitive reactivity to sad mood: Evidence from a correlational study and a non- randomized waiting list controlled study. Behavior Research and Therapy, 47, 623- 627.

Saltzman, A. (2011). Mindfulness: A guide for teachers. The Center for Contemplative Mind in Society. Retrieved from: http://www. contemplativemind. org/Mindfulness-A_Teachers_Guide. pdf.

Schmeichel, B. J., & Baumeister, R. F. (2004). Self-regulatory strength. In R. F. Baumeister & K. D. Vohs (Eds.), Handbook of self-regulation: Research, theory, and applications (pp. 84-98). New York: Guilford Press.

Segal, Z.V., Williams, J.M.G., & Teasdale, J.D. (2002). Mindfulness-based cognitive therapy for depression: a new approach to preventing relapse. New York: Guilford Press.

Sitaram, R., Ros, T., Stoeckel, L., Haller, S., Scharnowski, F., Lewis-Peacock, J., ... & Sulzer, J. (2017). Closed-loop brain training: the science of neurofeedback. Nature Reviews Neuroscience, 18(2), 86-100.

Shapiro, S. L., Astin, J. A., Bishop, S. R., & Cordova, M. (2005). Mindfulness-based stress reduction for health care professionals: Results from a randomized trial. International Journal of Stress Management, 12, 164 –176.

Sheldon, K. M., & Lyubomirsky, S. (2006). Achieving sustainable gains in happiness: Change your actions, not your circumstances. Journal of Happiness Studies, 7, 55-86.

Soekadar, S. R., Kohl, S. H., Mihara, M., & von Lühmann, A. (2021). Optical brain imaging and its application to neurofeedback. NeuroImage: Clinical, 30, 102577.

Soler, J., Valdepérez, A., Feliu-Soler, A., Pascual, J. C., Portella, M. J., Martín-Blanco, A., & ... Pérez, V. (2012). Effects of the dialectical behavioral therapy-mindfulness module on attention in patients with borderline personality disorder. Behaviour Research and Therapy, 50(2), 150-157.

Sundquist, J., Lilja, A., Palmér, K., Memon, A., Wang, X., Johansson, L. M., & Sundquist, K. (2015). Mindfulness group therapy in primary care patients with depression, anxiety and stress and adjustment disorders: randomized controlled trial. The British Journal of Psychiatry, 206(2), 128-135.

Tang, Y., Ma, Y., Wang, J., Fan, Y., Feng, S., Lu, Q., et al. (2007). Short-term meditation training improves attention and self-regulation. Proceedings of the National Academy of Sciences, 104, 17152–17156.

Tangney, J. P., Baumeister, R. F., & Boone, A. L. (2004). High self-control predicts good adjustment, less pathology, better grades, and interpersonal success. Journal of Personality, 72, 271–322.

Tapper, K., Shaw, C., Ilsley, J., Hill, A. J., Bond, F. W., & Moore, L. (2009). Exploratory randomised controlled trial of a mindfulness based weight loss intervention for women. Appetite, 52, 396–404.

Vansteenkiste, M., Ryan, R. M., & Deci, E. L. (2008). Self-determination theory and the explanatory role of psychological needs in human well-being. In L. Bruni, F. Comim, & M. Pugno (Eds.), Capabilities and happiness (pp. 187–223). Oxford: Oxford University Press.

Walach, H., Buchheld, N., Buttenmuller, V., Kleinknecht, N., & Schmidt, S. (2006). Measuring mindfulness: The Freiburg Mindfulness Inventory (FMI). Personality and Individual Differences, 40, 1543–1555.

Walker, L. J., & Pitts, R. C. (1998). Naturalistic conceptions of moral maturity.

Wayment, H.A., & Bauer, J.J. (2008). Transcending self-interest: Psychological explorations of the quiet ego. Washington, DC: American Psychological Association.

Wegner, D. M. (1994). Ironic processes of mental control. Psychological Review, 101, 34–52.

Westen, D. (1999). Psychology: Mind, brain, and culture (2nd ed). New York: Wiley.

Zeidan, F., Johnson, S.K., Diamond, B.J., David, Z. & Goolkasian, P. (2010). Mindfulness meditation improves cognition: evidence of brief mental training. Consciousness and cognition, 19, 597-605.

About the Author

Aida I. Askry is a philosopher who delicately intertwines philosophical insights with practical wisdom to explore the depths of human potential, peak performance, and the complexities of human experience.

With a Doctorate in Philosophy focusing on the mind-body connection and a specialization in Leadership and Organizational Development from Harvard Business School, Aida brings a unique and innovative perspective to personal development and systemic change.

Aida is celebrated for her creative and engaging interpretation of complex systems, providing pragmatic insights for those pursuing deep understanding in personal and professional spheres. Her distinctive style combines a playful approach to serious topics, making the exploration of developmental sciences and philosophy an enlightening and enjoyable journey.

You can learn more about Aida's programs and resources at www.holistech.club.

Also by the Author

20 Quests for your Journey Within
Aida I. Askry, PhD

Insight Job: 20 Quests for your Journey Within is a transformative exploration of self, offering a playful journey of expanded awareness and self-discovery.

Access a portal to broader horizons through enriching reflective journaling exercises and enlightening resources, all steeped in timeless wisdom. This versatile adventure fits in any schedule. Savor your personal evolution with each step, delving into 20 quests that can be explored in as little as fifteen minutes a day.

> "A helpful and sympathetic book, combining the theoretical with the practical in a fruitful way. Exercises that will help expand your consciousness and benefit your health, combined with an expanded, and according to my understanding, more true view of what a mysterious miracle consciousness really is than is found within conventional psychology."
>
> Review by Terje G. Simonsen
> Author of *Our Secret Powers: Telepathy, Clairvoyance and Precognition. A Short History of (Nearly) Everything Paranormal*